IT
BEGINS
WITH ME

Contents

Introduction

I have had the privilege of working with countless extraordinary people over the course of my career as a Master Certified Life Coach. My clients have endured a multitude of challenges, and it has been an honor to walk beside them in their journeys. Whether the nature of their challenges was interpersonal, financial, spiritual, or physical, I truly believe that even the most painful of these situations were absolutely created for their benefit. It is my contention that they endured such trials in order to grow in consciousness and become more mindful. These experiences have provided my clients with some of their most transformative learning, which is at the crux of every stride we take as human beings.

This book provides you with the opportunity to delve deeply, to challenge yourself, and to incorporate the insight you derive from it into your own life so you may venture beyond simply surviving and begin thriving in a life of joy and celebration. It has been gratifying, heartwarming, and enormously inspiring to witness the transformations that have taken place within my clients and their lives as a result of our work together. Clients who came to me with such intense self-discrimination that they wanted to crawl out of their own skin have come to accept, appreciate, and love themselves. I've watched resentments and passive-aggressive behavior melt away as my clients have become content and vastly more self-expressed. Individuals who felt unsafe in this world are now enjoying the unlimited freedom of trusting themselves to take care of themselves.

I wrote my first book, *Hairapy: Deeper than the Roots*, intending it to be used as a tool by my clients to complement our sessions together. Its purpose was to serve as a resource for greater comprehension while simultaneously providing them with consolation and support. The overall result was exactly what I had wanted: the readers no longer felt as though they were alone; they felt validated and empowered.

With more years of life coaching experience came more insight and inspiration. I employed these precious endowments to create the diagram that I call the "Michael Blomsterberg Life Coaching Enlightened Living Model", or "ELM" for short. I teach this model in my coaching and refer to it frequently. The impact that the ELM has had upon my clients has been extraordinary. It has brought them a tremendous amount of understanding and has been elemental in their development. Naturally, I began longing to extend those benefits beyond those who have access to me directly. Because I believe that my vision of a peaceful world becoming a reality begins with each of us, I decided to make this tool available to a global audience. So I carefully segmented the ELM and placed its elements into various chapters throughout this book. I wholeheartedly believe that this will bring you the maximum benefit of the ELM in the simplest, most relatable way. In essence, the journey that you are about to embark upon is a written version of the Michael Blomsterberg Life Coaching Enlightened Living Model.

Because I wanted your experience of the material to be as effortless as possible, this book was purposely composed to be poignant and succinct. The questions and exercises were well thought out and intentionally placed exactly where they are to move you along in your journey of self-discovery. The material will be most effective when digested slowly, in increments. This book is meant to be *experienced*, not "powered through". I wrote it such that each reader may go at his or her own pace. The best piece of advice that I can give you for approaching this book is to take a moment and sit with each chapter, question, and exercise. Please allow yourself the time to stop and ponder each of the questions, to let them permeate your being so that the answers and revelations may organically rise to your consciousness on their own. It's also a good idea to keep a journal nearby. A grey box on the page indicates that the contained material is an exercise. Any moment you feel inclined to journal into what you might be feeling, thinking, learning, or experiencing, please give yourself the permission to do so. You might even want to stop at the end of each chapter and write about what you took away from it. Doing so will only enhance this book's effectiveness. The degree to which you benefit from this book is completely dependent upon you.

It will likely be tremendously enlightening, as well, to pay attention to the ways in which your experience of this book parallels your experience of your life. For example, you might find yourself antsy, wanting to know where you're going or how to get there. Needing to know where you're going and needing to figure out how to get there do not always allow you to be present. Being fixated on a certain position can pull you out of the present moment and keep you locked in your limited analytical mind for years or even decades. This makes it challenging to relax into the journey, because you're constantly trying to get to a finish line. This book is not about getting to a certain destination. It is about allowing, accepting, and *surrendering*. It is meant to guide you into the deepest part of you, your truth. Please allow yourself to surrender into the experience, or if you're unable to do that, simply notice that, as well. It is only by being willing to simply go where your journey is taking you that your own, unique destination can be revealed.

Every individual will experience this book differently. The clues and directions for how to navigate your way are found in the questions, exercises, and guidance within this book. It is by going within and reflecting that your path reveals itself. Each answer and revelation that emerges will point you in the direction of the next one. As you complete each leg of your journey, you'll be able to feel the effects at your core and see them transcending into your daily life. With more knowledge, you will create more possibilities for yourself. By venturing deeper within, you will reacquaint with your true, authentic self. Befriending your true self will reflexively allow you to have more compassion and love for you. This unification will shift your life dramatically.

You are very special and very important. This, I promise. Thank you for being you, exactly as you are. My intention for writing this book is that all who read it begin to open their hearts to themselves without condition. I want you to know that you're neither alone nor crazy. Whatever you're going through and wherever you are in your life, my hope is for you to feel loved and validated as a human being, in who you are, in your entire existence. My hope is that you feel safe in a world that very often doesn't make sense, that you comprehend (at the center of your being) how beautiful and remarkable you truly are. This way, you have supreme access to your resourcefulness and your creative power so that you manifest all that you desire in your life. May this book inspire and empower you. May you come to remain in a state of peacefulness within yourself that transcends into the world around you. May you live being the person that you were destined to be.

I

Unveiling
The True You

Every one of us learns how to act by observing those living examples in the world around us. We determine how to address others, what manners to use at the dinner table, and what not to say to Mom when she's in a bad mood. As we grow up, we begin to figure out ways of going about getting the things that we want. For many of us, what we desire most is to know that we matter, to be a part of the whole, to be included. We often deduce that, in order for this to occur, we should act, behave, and simply *be* a certain way. We infer from our experiences, both with our families and society, that it is necessary for us to deny part (or all) of our true selves in order to be accepted and that we must abandon our voice in order to belong. We teach ourselves, for example, that people will not get upset with us for disagreeing with them as long as we keep quiet about our opinions.

Or perhaps we learn that people seem to like us more if we do everything in our power to accommodate them. Maybe we conclude that we need to bully others in order to get our way. In reality, we might be opinionated, unable or unwilling to accommodate, or gentle, but we've adopted ways of being that are inauthentic for ourselves, because we thought that we needed to do so in order to fit in and to survive in our world. Other times, we bend ourselves into pretzels when we find ourselves attracted to someone in an attempt to be whom we think that person might want. My concern is that, by altering our personalities to fit in, we leave ourselves feeling empty and barren. Rather than honoring our own values, staying true to ourselves, and expressing ourselves freely and directly, we often confine ourselves to a set of rules about how we should behave. Thus, we end up feeling resentful and acting as an imposter. We are creating a world around our *projected* image and, therefore, a life that is out of alignment with our truth and integrity. How does it feel when you silence your own voice, because you don't think that it is as important or relevant as someone else's?

When you do this, the people in your life end up in a relationship with the person that you're presenting yourself to be in place of the real you. This leaves us feeling trapped and fraudulent, having deserted our true nature in that masquerade. In this disconnect, we get snared in our people-pleasing thoughts of trying to anticipate others' responses or second-guessing their reactions to the image we've presented to them. This can leave us feeling vacant and riddled with anxiety. I know that we all have ideas of what is or is not appealing and who or what we'd rather be in order to win the approval of others. Do you really prefer to be someone other than who you are? In denying your true nature by putting on façades, you dilute that very luminous essence that you innately possess. Can you see how dimming your own light makes it challenging to have an authentic exchange?

Doesn't it seem so simple that we should be and act as we are at our core? Why, then, do we orchestrate the dances that we do as diversions from our true selves? Why do we resist our inherent nature and force ourselves to put on façades? How can we attract what we want and be appreciated for who we really are if we hide our authentic selves from everyone, including us? How can we live a joyous life if we're acting as though we're someone else, with our pretense overshadowing our authenticity?

If we were able to stop trying to be what we think we should, to shed the façade, and to begin to accept and embrace the unique facets of our own personality, we would shine as brightly as we were meant to shine. We would like ourselves and even enjoy our own company. This would be so much more pleasurable and fulfilling, because this loving would permeate into all of our life's experiences. We would then be available to unconditionally share ourselves with others and live much richer lives as the spiritual beings that we truly are.

When we can get out of our own way and revere the distinct characteristics and qualities that we presently embody, we can then zestfully unveil ourselves to the world and begin to relish a life that is consistent with our true nature. Having our own unbridled approval enables us to fully accept ourselves, as we are; to fully *like* ourselves without condition; and to enjoy ourselves beyond measure. By eliminating our self-inflicted inhibitions and constraints, we untether ourselves so that we may take flight and soar. We no longer question others' acceptance of us, because we know that they're not interacting with an imposter anymore. In revealing our honest selves to us and to the world, we begin to attract people and experiences that are consistent with who we *truly* are. Our authenticity is more potent than we could ever imagine.

2

LET THE
EVOLUTION BEGIN

One principle that continues to prove itself to me is that life keeps "life-ing". In other words, life is the way it is, and it continues to unfold as it does. It always has; it always will. Our journeys present some difficult challenges. However, it's our nonacceptance and rigid positions that create our reactions to them, which can bring us deep upset, anger, resentment, and a host of other feelings. These reactions are important, vital teachers that help us to notice ourselves, what needs to be addressed, and what triggers those emotional "buttons" of which we're not fully conscious yet. They are interventions in the course and the direction of our lives. I think of such experiences as "God shining light on my blind spots", and I believe God is frequently doing this for me. Shining light on what once troubled you will allow you to now be freed from it and enlightened by it instead. Once-dormant sadness, fear, pain, guilt, shame, and anger are now invited to enter your consciousness. These feelings rise up within you so that they may be released. They no longer belong to you so you no longer need to house them. This allows you to become a clean and open vessel. As you allow yourself to feel your feelings, you create more understanding for them. Give yourself the grace to consciously experience and accept these feelings, and they will begin melting away. In your ability to lean into them, you've already begun to heal. I'm grateful that God keeps shining light on my blind spots, because it allows me more freedom, possibility, and mobility on this planet.

Throughout my life's experiences, I've found that a great sense of my peace lies in being able to be with as many different fear-based feelings as I can from an observational, non-judgmental, neutral, and accepting place within myself. The more that I can be with my feelings, the less they will cage and own me. The less they cage and own me, the less power they have over me. Many people attempt to ignore these feelings, hoping that they will go away. That is not how it works. Bringing awareness to all that is happening inside of ourselves is paramount; it is life-giving. It is actually by giving our feelings a voice that they begin dissolving on their own. Trust this.

Please allow your feelings to flow freely; to be experienced, expressed, and released. Please do your best to accept your feelings, and try not to argue with or judge your feelings or yourself for having them. I know that you are human and that this is a tall order. If having certain feelings upsets you or feels uncomfortable, see if you can just bring acceptance to that fact. The more I allow myself to experience my feelings in this way, the more they continue to dissipate, and the more I am liberated to ascend in my life. As their power over me subsides, they lose their charge and are no longer a trigger. The less of a trigger they are, the less of a reaction I have. As I have less of a reaction, I am more present to love and be loved, which makes me a safer person to be around.

By accepting myself for who I am, I am then able to accept others for who *they* are. A brotherhood is formed that transcends onto our planet. As more and more people begin to accept themselves (and thus others), we will witness a growing global transformation of people appreciating, and even celebrating, one another's uniqueness and diversity.

Always know that whatever is happening within us is simply providing great information for us to learn more about ourselves, to grow, and to live with a higher level of consciousness. This affords us more peace and understanding in our lives. All feelings are happening for our personal development. There's nothing to fear. Our feelings can be our greatest teachers. May you one day be able to befriend and to revel in each and every one.

Please remember as you embark upon this journey that there is no right way or wrong way. There's only the perfect way, and whichever way you choose is perfect for this time and place on your path. I just ask that you be as nurturing with yourself as you can be, *at all times*. Please be respectful of you.

3

THE LOVE
THAT YOU ARE

A good friend of mine has an incredible cherry cobbler recipe. She's made that heavenly delight so many times over the years that she has perfected it. The crust is simultaneously rich and flaky, and the cherries are always the perfect blend of sweet and tart. I've heard countless people remark that they could "live on" her cobbler. Yes, it's that good. Now, let's say that her cherry cobbler represents God, the universe, spirit, energy, or whatever you call your higher power (the whole from which we all originated). Though we might have different definitions or terms for our higher power, they all are embodiments of a divine consciousness, of a divine intelligence. Our higher power is omnipotent and whole. It is the essence of pure, unconditional love; just as my friend's cherry cobbler is sweet, flaky, rich, and delicious. If my friend were to cut a slice of the cobbler and give it to you, that slice would be just as delectable as the whole cobbler from which it came. So by this rationale, if you come from a higher power with all those amazing attributes, how could you be any different than the whole? If your higher power is love, then it only makes sense that you are that love, too. If your higher power is perfect, then everything it sprouts must be perfect, as well. If your higher power possesses beauty, then that same beauty lies within you. This is the same for every single person on this planet.

As human beings, we've learned to look at our feelings, our emotions, our thoughts, our concepts, and our behaviors as good or bad, positive or negative, right or wrong. Many of us label joy, for instance, as positive; while we label sadness as negative. Gratitude is good, while anxiety is bad. Acceptance is right, while hostility is wrong. However, if we have spawned from the collective whole that is our higher power, then that would mean that every thought or feeling that we experience or behavior that we display would also have to be perfect as it is. Thus, none of our feelings *could* be wrong or bad. They would simply be other parts of us, and of that perfect whole – dimmer or darker shades of love. Regardless of which part of us created the feeling (e.g., our ego or our higher self), everything would have to come from our higher power. Therefore, everything would have to be necessary, right, and meant to be at certain junctures in our development. Living in this knowledge is freedom.

If we separate our feelings and emotions into categories of things we believe we should or should not feel, we are destined to punish ourselves, think poorly of ourselves, and put ourselves down whenever we feel something that we consider to be bad. In this self-condemnation, we really make life hard for ourselves. Many of us become walking apologies. We end up with poor self-images, because we've attached who we think we are (our identities) to those feelings that we perceive as objectionable or shameful. We believe that we are those feelings that we judge and measure as bad or wrong. Thus, we believe that, because we have these feelings, there's something "wrong" with us. This concept of unworthiness becomes our core belief about ourselves. Thus, we enter each new day with the presumption that we're "bad" people. *There's nothing wrong with us.* It's as though we've forgotten that we are that scrumptious cherry cobbler, and we've begun to think of ourselves as three-day old, stale bread instead. That feeling of unworthiness permeates from within us onto and into everything we do and say. Sure, we try to hide it, but it still makes its way to the surface, just like a Whac-a-Mole game. We end up feeling unworthy of ourselves and therefore feeling unworthy of our feelings, as well, be they feelings of happiness or despair. Yet if we can cease the labeling and associating of everything we feel as either "good" or "bad", we can see our feelings for what they really are: simple emotions. I believe that it is necessary for us to have access to both those emotions that we deem good *and* those that we deem not so good so that we can feel all of our feelings, rather than clinging to the "good" ones and stifling the "bad" while living half of a life. Those "bad" emotions are essential for us to accept and embrace in order to heal and ascend, whereby we get to live a life of wholeness, presence, dignity, and freedom. Denial of those feelings condemns us to self-imposed emotional prisons. Here's a fun fact: not allowing ourselves the permission to feel the "bad" ones also cuts off our circulation from feeling the "good" ones, as well. This is not healthy. For me, it is much more empowering to allow myself to experience uncomfortable or undesirable emotions than to bottle them up and let them fester inside of me or attempt to evade them. Permitting myself to feel what I'm actually feeling instead of resisting it frees me from that self-imposed incarceration and gives me back my life. It's like getting the skeleton key to my cell. It is by honoring all of our emotions and feeling all that we need to feel that we liberate ourselves. It is by clearing all of our emotional sludge that we come back to the remembrance of the love that we truly are.

4

DIVING IN

There are many reasons why we unconsciously create our own emotional prisons. One of the most common is that we believe our frightened mind's claims that if we are honest, vulnerable, or direct we can be hurt or left or that we might hurt or offend another. This puts us in an adversarial relationship with our truthfulness. In addition, it puts our trust with ourselves into question. This explains why we keep (or at least we think we keep) certain emotions off limits or at bay. We have negative associations with people who express those emotions, or we're just afraid of whatever it is that our frightened mind (which is our ego) tells us might happen if we allow ourselves to express them. So many of us barricade our hearts for this very reason. We wonder why we feel so isolated and alone. We've segregated ourselves. In addition, many of us are simply unconscious as to what we are actually experiencing within. Certain emotions feel bigger than us, as if they are an abyss that will engulf and never release us if we allow ourselves to experience them. I understand what that feels like, but the reality is that it is just not possible. These emotions can seem so daunting and overwhelming that we find it incredibly difficult to trust ourselves to be able to face them. However, feeling content and safe in this world necessitates us facing those emotions. Let's begin by trusting that we're a piece of a perfect whole and that we would never be given more than we can handle.

When we identify ourselves by our fear-based feelings, many of us believe that we literally *are* those emotions. How is that possible? Just because you feel sad in one moment or angry in another, it doesn't mean that you're a sad or angry person. When we believe that, we tend to desperately grasp onto any tangible method of evaluating ourselves that we can find. We identify with characteristics and qualities in the external, physical world; attach meaning and connotation to them; and define ourselves through our possessions, our bank accounts, what we do, what we look like, our accomplishments and accolades (or lack thereof), what other people think of us, our history, and our current story. We compare those aspects of our lives to those of others, and we weigh and measure until we think we know exactly where we stand in the world: where we're right, where we're wrong, who we are, who we aren't, what we deserve, and what we don't deserve. Our black and white perspective places us in a hierarchical world where some people are above us, and others are below us, and where we're constantly comparing ourselves to everyone else and thus confining ourselves within the walls of that hell. We have identities that parallel how we feel about ourselves and where we think we fit into the world. It's insane. That identity then mandates that we limit ourselves, suppress our creativity, repress our personality, punish ourselves, and create hardships for ourselves. We project this identity for others to see, and they follow our lead and treat us accordingly. It's a vicious, cyclical pattern.

Residing within this emotional torture chamber while we spend our days doubting and worrying is indicative of the fact that we've made *fear* our higher power. We've lost our awareness of our true selves, and we're allowing our frightened mind to call the shots. From this place, our higher power can be judgmental, critical, condemning, and punishing. I have lived with fear as my higher power for the majority of my years, and let me tell you – when that is happening, my journey is arduous. I've drowned myself in a perpetual state of worry and anxiety by constantly obsessing over everything, but by always posturing as if all was well and I was okay. It wasn't until recently that I realized that living in a perpetual state of anxiety was my modus operandi. For many years, my life was riddled with distrust. Now, however, my higher power (more often than not) is compassionate, nurturing, merciful, and loving. I have faith that all is *always* as it should be. As I've grown in my awareness of my goodness, I've come to authentically recognize the divinity within me and realize that I have a good heart. I now know that I am made in God's image and likeness, cut from the same cloth, beautiful, perfect, and whole just as I am. I am – we all are – connected to that divinity, that *love*, twenty-four/seven; it is what we are. We are love, and that is that. Loving is our natural state. When we are not being loving, we impose duress upon ourselves. We cannot lose the love that we are; it is inherent in our being. We can only temporarily lose our *cognizance* of it when our frightened mind's limiting perceptions divert us elsewhere.

Many people do not understand that access to their emotions is the road to emancipation. Remaining open to each and every emotion allows for our feelings to flow through us without getting lodged inside of us. It allows us to be clean, available, and uncluttered so we can awaken to our divine magnificence. This is what leaves us accessible for true choice. Access to everything we feel is our passage to true choice. As we remain open, willing, and present, we're not burdened by any of the emotional toxicity that dulls our receptivity. We're unobstructed. Living from our frightened mind's skewed self-image with limited access to our emotions means denying ourselves true choice. When people cut themselves off from any part of their emotions, decisions are spawned out of their fearful reactions. They think, in their robotic unconsciousness, that they're making choices, but I beg to differ. Actual choices can only be made by someone who is highly conscious and mindful, meaning that their heart and their mind are open, receptive, and working together. That's when we possess the power of choice.

This concept has taken me many years to fully understand. It wasn't until I allowed myself the permission to embrace and explore some of my fear-based feelings that I realized that the denying, ignoring, or suppressing of them had obstructed my view and cognition of my true magnificence by casting an overlay, a sludge or film if you will, which made it impossible for me to recognize my divine nature. I'm now clear that, when I'm present, I'm at my best. And when I'm at my best, I'm connected to that part of myself which I refer to as my "higher self". This connection grants me access to true, conscious choice, as I'm no longer unconsciously walking around, reacting to life and circumstances.

5

LIMITLESS OPTIONS

Please take a moment to bring to mind a person in your life whom you might have judged (or are still judging) based upon how they live their life, the circumstances in their life, or how you feel they are being treated. I bring this to mind, because this is very important to me, as I feel that a lot of people are being dismissed due to our unconsciousness and righteousness. I feel as though they need our compassion and understanding, rather than our incrimination and judgment. For example, no one who is connected to their higher self would *choose* to be beaten or consciously allow themself to be violated. So a decision to stay with an abuser, for instance, would have to be based in some type of fear, where one is not connected to their higher self. Perhaps those who decide to remain in such situations are afraid of losing what they know to be love or attention, or they're worried about their financial situation. Perhaps their religion doesn't allow for divorce. Maybe they fear they're not good enough, smart enough, pretty enough, capable enough. So who else would want them? They could be afraid of losing a victim identity or a doormat identity. Who would they be now? How would they relate to others? Perhaps they do not know how to operate in a world without mayhem or chaos. They might even be afraid to be alone. We act as if we know what's going on in their lives, but do we really? Fear, especially fear of the unknown, has proven to be paralyzing and debilitating for numerous people. For many, the fear of tearing apart their family and feeling that the decision to end a relationship could ruin their children's lives are what keep them in bondage to their abusive situations. The inhumane conditions that people will endure when they're living unconsciously are incomprehensible. At the same time, the evil acts being inflicted upon the abused, for instance, are also likely to be byproducts of fearfulness. Since everyone is love at their core, such acts can only be executed by someone who has lost the awareness of their true, divine nature and who has become a victim of their own pain and limitations. Once again, the antidote is conscious connection to the love that we are, the love that sources us. That connection alters our perspective and frame of mind so that we may live in a peaceful state with access to clear options. This state of connection is so overpowering that it can put an end to even the most abhorrent behavior.

Those living *presently* in their lives would never choose hardship, struggle, indignity, or ill-treatment. They would choose joy, compassion, safety, ease. It's really a no-brainer. For it is in this unconditional space that we find our decisions to be based in consciousness, self-respect, and loving kindness (toward ourselves). The power of choice avails itself when we're walking with our higher power.

6

POSITIVELY
AUTHENTIC

Today, many people are enduring trying times. The economy is struggling, and so is a large part of the world's population. Amid these circumstances, I often hear people say, "Just be positive". *Just be positive about the money you've lost. Just be positive about your termination at the bank. Just be positive about the future.* I hear it all the time, and I understand it. I think it's healthy as long as you're allowing yourself to stay true to what you're feeling in the moment. Forcing any type of inauthentic attitude upon oneself can create deep agony in the future.

If I've recently discovered a dark secret about my spouse, or if I'm enduring cancer treatments (as I have in the past), or if I've suffered the loss of a loved one, for example, I am going to be hosting a myriad of feelings. When others tell me to be positive, I find it to be very dismissing and invalidating of what I'm experiencing. I know in my heart that they're just trying to be loving and supportive; yet it feels as though I'm being indirectly told to deny the hurt, fear, sadness, or other feelings that are accompanying my experience. By buying into the notion that I should stay positive, I can end up negating emotions that are deemed bad, wrong, or negative. Those dismissed feelings, of course, only knock louder and louder to be heard, wreaking havoc on my life and thus chipping away at my well-being. I've now set myself up to be self-defeating whenever I engage in any thoughts, behaviors, or actions that don't qualify as "positive". I then become a victim of myself when I am unable to sustain that false state of positivity. My belief that I'm letting myself down or burdening others by not remaining optimistic then plagues my days. Within this spiral, no matter how hard I try to let go of the thoughts and feelings around what I'm experiencing, it simply isn't possible. For me, there's no way out when I'm inauthentically trying to be positive.

Many of my clients ask me how they can get around the fear, stop the fear, let go of the fear, or not have fear in such situations. I tell them that the good news is that they're conscious of the fact that the fear is there. That's the win. However, escaping the fear is not the answer. *Befriending* the fear is the answer. We want no enemies, not even fear. When faced with this type of circumstance, I'm going to allow myself to feel whatever I'm feeling, regardless of whether those feelings are fear, doubt, worry, or otherwise. I permit myself to stay authentic to whatever I'm currently feeling at any given moment. When I grant myself access to every feeling, "good" *and* "bad", my energy is no longer concentrated on resisting or evading the "bad" feelings. Instead, the thoughts that are leading to those feelings begin to come into focus. Once I'm aware of the thoughts that are causing my feelings, I can address what's *really* taking place within me. The very act of allowing, without reservation, hesitation, or judgment, is an act of self-love. Authorizing myself to accept the reality of how I'm feeling is life-giving. Through the observation of my actions and reactions, I learn and grow. There's a lot to be said for turning around and facing your fear, examining it, allying with it, learning from it, and welcoming it as much as you can. It's then that those uncomfortable thoughts and feelings begin to lessen. When I look my feelings in the eye, they lose their power and begin to slip away. When I acknowledge and accept them, their grip loosens, and they begin to let go of me. In this recognition, I create greater understanding with myself, for myself, and about myself. By being kind with myself in this manner, I get to live a far more fulfilling and joyful life.

7

Peel The Labels

We now get to intervene in our own plights. In the observation of your thoughts, feelings, and behavior, begin to notice your reaction to criticism. Why do you think that criticism can hurt so much? When someone feels a certain way or thinks, says, or implies something about you that is contrary to the image you're trying to project, the comment hurts, because it feels unkind, unwarranted, and disrespectful; but it hurts also because a part of you might believe or fear that it is true. Many of you have been doing everything in your power to hide, deny, and conceal this from yourselves, possibly for years. So when this trigger is acknowledged, it can create quite a sting within you. I refer to this concept as "think/feel/say", and I ask my clients, *Which adjectives or opinions conjure an adverse reaction within you when someone thinks, feels, or says them about you?* Come on out, liberate yourself. Can you be truthful and flush out your "self-bias" so that your true, authentic self can emerge? What are you concealing from yourself? What is it that you need to know about you? When you can honestly answer these questions, you get to exhale and relax into your life again. Pay attention to how you feel when such things are said or thought about you. Notice how often you say them about yourself. What if people are following your lead and treating you the way you treat yourself? By identifying what you don't want people to think about you, you're also identifying what you're trying to prove to yourself about yourself. They are one and the same. For example, if you don't want people to think that you are stupid, I'm sure that you spend most of your days out there trying to prove how smart, able, and capable you are. Some of you will even be out there pointing out how stupid you think you sometimes are, through your own commentary about your actions. It works both ways. For many years, my Achilles' heel was the term "selfish". Every second of every day was spent trying to prove that I wasn't selfish. From the time that I got up until the time I went to bed, countless hours of energy were used to do generous, kind, selfless acts to prove to myself that I wasn't selfish, as I had been told I was as a child. For me, this meant that I was a good person. These are the kinds of thoughts and concepts that define and limit our world. They are the confinements that fuel poor self-image and that keep us feeling bad about ourselves. They drive us to incessantly look outside of ourselves for something to fill that void inside and to make us feel better.

By identifying those labels that we adhere to that keep us unaware of our higher selves, we can begin to look at the payoff that we receive for hosting them. What is it that you get out of carrying around all of that dense toxicity all of the time? Please take a moment to sit with this. Do you get a license to act out; to live in misery; to gain people's sympathy and win over their affections; to dislike yourself; to feel misunderstood; to feel separate, and thus falsely safe in the world? What is it? I ask, because you are important, and you deserve goodness. I feel like so many people on this planet have little to no true sense of themselves. Most have adopted a false identification and are toiling to solidify that persona. We spend countless hours trying to prove or disprove that we are or aren't something: special, important, worth less, unworthy, wise, attractive, unattractive. Or, we're trying to prove that we're better than this person or nothing like that person. We demonstrate this in a myriad of ways, from our actions to our nonverbal communication. Can you see how this affects the quality of your life?

The limitations of attaching to an identity leave us with no space to grow, expand, or evolve. There is only the confinement of trying to groom and maintain a false, projected image. Please don't encapsulate yourself. There's no need to tie yourself into knots to protect some false, manufactured persona. Can we not just allow others to have their opinions about us? Isn't your opinion about you what matters most?

8

ENDORSING YOU

When we seek approval from others, it is most often an attempt to prove something to ourselves. Usually we're trying to prove that we're "somebody", that we're worth keeping around, that we're a good person, or that we're lovable. If we believe that there is something wrong with us, we believe that others see it, too. We assume that others are thinking the same things about us that we're thinking about ourselves. So when we judge ourselves, we think that other people are judging us for the same reason. It's all our projection. I'm certain that most people's focus lies elsewhere. Likewise, if we can get others to approve of us, we feel okay about ourselves for about fifteen seconds. The lengths that we'll go to in our attempts to manipulate others' views of us when we're jonesing for validation are astounding.

Once we've gained the approval of others, why is it

that we're often still not content? Because we continue to lack *our own* approval. Since we don't even feel deserving of our approval, others' approval will never suffice. You see, once again, we know that we're pretending to be someone other than who we see ourselves to be in a crafty attempt to control people's impressions of us in order to gain their approval. It's one giant, pretentious circus. We know that their approval is not for us, but rather for the persona we've presented, so it doesn't feel real. They're endorsing an imposter. Due to our feeling inadequate, we have a hard time believing and receiving that acknowledgment. In addition, because we usually operate with an agenda of trying to win over the affections of others, we think that other people are doing the same, so we grow leery. We end up not trusting and being suspicious of others and their agendas. In constantly questioning the intentions of others, we live a guarded existence. It's exhausting to wander aimlessly without the approval of the one source from which we really require it – ourselves.

When we become emotionally dependent upon others to determine our worth, we can become burdens both to them and to ourselves. We can't really rely on ourselves to "stamp our own passports", so to speak, so we rely on others to essentially be our dispensaries for love, validation, and recognition. This is too much responsibility to place upon another human being. When we stop attempting to procure love and approval from others and start to give it to ourselves, our lives shift dramatically. Nourishing ourselves in this way, we begin to recognize the beauty that lies within us and fall deeply *in like* with ourselves. Never again do we need to abandon ourselves for validation from another.

By not seeking approval outside of ourselves, we get to turn inward. As we venture inside, we discover that we never needed other people's approval. What we've been looking for is our own, and what we have always had is that of our higher power's. We find comfort and relief in this unwavering constant. Wholeheartedly approving of ourselves eliminates our need to forage for and cling to affection from outside sources. When we have our own approval, we don't need to seek it elsewhere. We begin to relish our uniqueness, validating ourselves. In addition, we begin to understand that other people aren't really approving or disapproving of *us*, but that they are, in actuality, approving or disapproving of their *perception* of us. This is a vast difference.

What are the ways in which you can be more kind and approving of yourself in this very moment? Enjoy the confidence and contentment that come with having your own endorsement.

9

Fact Or Fiction?

We all have lectures, narratives, or anecdotes that we silently speak to ourselves internally in an effort to make sense of life. We believe that we know these things to be true because of our past experiences. However, in reality they are often just concepts that position us in opposition to ourselves, others, and life. Due to our rigid stance of having to be right about, well, most everything, we set ourselves up to have adversaries. In addition, being right means that we better understand how life works, that we definitively know how it should and shouldn't be. Do we really? We have set these axioms in place so that we know how to operate and navigate our way through life. We believe that we are safe within this perimeter. Let's be honest, though. Are we safe, or are we *confined*? *I'll never get married. Everyone takes advantage of me. I can't lose weight. Anyone I love will eventually leave me.* Adhering to and using these concepts as justifications limits what we will allow to be possible in our lives. So in reality, these stories are actually restraining us by closing us off from the generosity that life has to offer.

What inner commentary is dictating your life? Notice if it offers you a life of opportunities and prosperity or a life of lack and scarcity. What are you consistently telling yourself? Is it that you're a failure; that you can't trust people; or that it's too late and you've missed your chance? Maybe you think that things don't work out for you, because you're fat, short, gay, or a minority. There are endless theories that we subscribe to as though they were facts. We inhabit them and then build our lives around their assumed premises. Please pay attention to your internal narratives, for they are ruling your life. They are determining your quality of life and your levels of intimacy, connection, and happiness. How much longer do you want a life consistent with those limiting perceptions and beliefs? The world in which you currently reside is a mirror image of your internal thoughts.

Perhaps it is time to peer underneath these beliefs and perceptions. This will require great willingness, courage, and honesty. Begin by asking yourself: *How does adhering to this belief serve me? What do I get out of subscribing to it? What is my reward for housing it? What is my payoff for harboring it? Does this tenet limit or liberate me?* Maybe this belief serves you by giving you an alibi for not trying or putting yourself out there. Perhaps what you're getting out of it is shelter, protection, or self-preservation. Maybe your reward is approval, sympathy, or attention. Could your motivation be that you get to fit in and feel accepted? Could *suffering* be your payoff? Maybe you get to be right and, thus, feel superior. For me, looking at my accountability in the whole of my life (in relationships with others and in all situations) keeps my side of the fence clean. I find my accountability by examining my actions, beliefs, motivations, and reasoning. Once I identify my part in a situation, I'm no longer at the effect of the person or ordeal. Serving myself in this proactive manner puts the power back in my hands. I'm no longer waiting for people to make the first move, to make it better, to make me feel good, or to be different. Nor am I sitting around expecting the situation to change. In addition, by not vilifying another, I'm no longer victimizing myself. Thus, my healing, movement, and emancipation have already begun. Do you want to be right? Or do you want to live a full, rich, and satisfying life?

As we become aware of our thoughts, regardless of what they are, we become more present, conscious, and cognizant of the stories that we tell ourselves in our minds. If our stories contradict our present reality, then it is essential to remember that *they're mere tales of fiction* fabricated by our frightened minds. They're not true, but our frightened minds will tell us that they're true. Your frightened mind will stop at nothing to keep you in servitude to it, to keep you coming back for more. It will tell you things like: *this shouldn't be happening; this shouldn't be happening to me; they should just stop what they're doing; I didn't sign up for this; I shouldn't have to go through crap like this.* Now that you understand what is happening, you no longer need to feed your frightened mind's veracious appetite by agreeing with its content. And FYI, if something is happening, based on the factual basis that it is, then it's supposed to be happening, because it is. The more we pay attention to these inner narratives that oppose our current circumstances, the more we begin to notice the uncomfortable feelings that accompany them. These distressing thoughts generate feelings of anxiety, disappointment, shame, guilt, resentment, rage, and a host of so many others. As you connect the dots, you will begin to see how your troubling thoughts directly correlate to those painful, and often immobilizing, feelings.

As always, it is immensely empowering to welcome those thoughts and feelings, to open ourselves to what we're really experiencing. For it is when we acknowledge and accept the undesirable emotions that they lose their power. It's like the monster in the closet when you're a child. The more afraid of it you are, and the more you hide from it, the scarier it becomes. Yet when you're ready to open the closet, peek inside, acknowledge what's actually there, and accept it for what it is, that monster loses its power over you, and those fearful feelings begin to slip away. Giving your encumbering thoughts and feelings a voice allows you to be released from their captivity. The opportunity is always there for you to surrender and lean into whatever you're resisting.

Please stay highly conscious as to which thoughts you are in agreement with, because those agreements determine your quality of life. In other words, stay alert to what kind of life you are perpetuating for yourself by giving certain ideas your stamp of approval, for they become self-fulfilling prophecies. Without our internal narratives holding us captive, we open up a new world of possibilities for ourselves. The power lies within your reach.

10

ULTERIOR MOTIVES

There are feelings that we relish, there are those that we don't mind experiencing, and then there are the feelings that we'd prefer never to admit that we have, even to ourselves. Many of us would like to be thought of as giving, generous, and caring. We'd rather not be looked at as selfish, petty, or stingy. Sometimes, in our efforts to prove that we embody those favorable attributes, we'll go so far as to constantly accommodate or please others. We do this at our own expense, even when it doesn't feel honest or authentic for us to do so. We believe that this will ensure that we are deemed "good" (i.e., a good parent, a good friend, or a good person). To maintain this appearance we will often act in fallaciously over-kind and over-generous manners. We allow ourselves to be overly accessible, permitting others to call upon us for anything at any time, often to the point where other people depend upon us to get through their day. We make ourselves as integral and as indispensable as possible, secretly attempting to control how others feel about us. Not only does this give us a function in life, but we honestly believe that this ensures that we will always be needed and thus never tossed aside or left behind. This brings us great comfort. Our motives, seemingly altruistic, are often packed with hidden agenda. Now is the time to tell the truth. Please take a moment to notice if your motives are altruistic and clean or if they are self-serving and tainted. If they are not pure, then what does that cost you? What happens to the true, authentic you every time you do something in order to bait and hook another's favor?

Many of us give to others, expecting that they will respect, value, appreciate, or love us in return. Our expectations make our generosity conditional. Can you see the strings attached in this equation? We're silently saying: *I'm going to give to you, but there's something that you need to give me in return.* When we make our giving conditional, but make it appear as if it's unconditional, we set ourselves up to experience a lot of disappointment, blame, and hurt. The people in our lives think that we're being forthright and upstanding so they act accordingly. They do not understand the rules of the manipulative game that we've entered into with them, nor do they even know that they're a participant. This is our doing. Isn't it twisted? We begin to resent those to whom we're giving when we believe that they're not appreciating our valiant efforts. In addition, we become incensed and indignant when we feel as though our giving is a one-way street with no reciprocity. However, isn't it our feelings of inadequacy and unworthiness that are calling the shots? Doesn't this make it challenging for us to receive? We're not available. So where would there be any room for anyone to give to us? We're at a stalemate. We set this up brilliantly. These people are serving as a diversion from something about ourselves that we're not quite ready to face yet. They're giving us a brief reprieve by allowing us to temporarily use them as a distraction from what's happening inside of us. Yes, we're using others to soothe ourselves and to fill our own voids.

What lengths will you go to in order to keep people in your life or to avoid dealing with your own issues or being alone? Will you give and give and give until you're exhausted, resentful, and upset with yourself? Will you give until you have nothing left to give? If so, what effect does this have upon your wellness? It's time to be honest about your motives and agenda. Your character and integrity depend upon it. It's time to pull your own covers so that you finally have a say in what you're doing. Imagine what it will feel like knowing that you can count on you to be authentic in all your deeds.

11

ME FIRST

Having needs doesn't make you needy; it makes you human. Being emotionally unavailable to oneself and unconsciously placing our needs upon others to fulfill is what makes one seem "needy". Looking outside of ourselves to fulfill those needs means placing impossible expectations on others and then being stuck with the aftermath of disappointment when they can't meet them. It's really a very simple formula. The good news is that this disappointment is something you bring upon yourself. So this is something that you can alter. *You're* responsible for the disappointment that you feel. You have a say in whether you want to look to others to meet your needs (and we know where that can lead) or whether you would rather look to yourself. One way is painful, while the other way is peaceful. Choosing the peaceful route affords us the opportunity to cease blaming everyone else for our discontent and reclaim responsibility for our own care and happiness.

In the process of learning to take care of ourselves, boundaries are essential. Setting boundaries, for me, is another way of being loving toward myself. They keep me honest. My boundaries represent what's true for me; what isn't true for me; what works for me; what doesn't work for me; what feels right for me; what doesn't feel right for me; what feels appropriate to me; and what doesn't feel appropriate to me. That's it. They're not personal, nor are they to punish or teach a lesson. They are about what best takes care of me.

For some of us, it might be necessary now to limit our previously gratuitous generosity and become authentically generous with ourselves by implementing boundaries. This means having to say no, risk being unpopular, and risk others being disappointed. I know that that might be challenging for many of you. However, the honor and dignity that accompanies our truthfulness is priceless. In addition, I think it may be helpful to make the distinction between setting boundaries from a loving place versus constructing barriers from fear. For instance, let's say that your sister always asks you to make your famous Bolognese sauce for family gatherings. It's delicious, but it takes hours and costs a small fortune to make. On a particularly busy Thursday afternoon, she sends an email requesting the sauce for an impromptu Saturday dinner. Last-minute requests from her are not an uncommon occurrence. You might be tempted to respond with something like, "Doesn't anyone else ever contribute? I have a life, you know. My time is valuable, too. You can't keep asking me to do things at the last minute. I'm not giving up another Saturday because you have to have Bolognese." A more beneficial, bridging way to set the same boundary would be to say, "I am really flattered that you enjoy my sauce that much, and I love being able to make it for everyone. Unfortunately, I won't be able to make it this time. I'd prefer to have more advance notice next time. I look forward to seeing you on Saturday." It's really as simple as that. It's not that complicated. It's just about you being honest about what feels right for you. That's it. It's never necessary to make someone an enemy. A loving boundary unites, where a fearful barrier divides. One is amicable; the other sparks conflict.

Please remind yourself that setting boundaries in order to take care of yourself is not selfish; it is simply *self-care*. It's a way of being loving with ourselves. It's okay to take care of you first. Actually, it's recommended. When setting a boundary, you might want to ask yourself: *What is the most honest and respectful way to take care of myself in this situation?*

12

SIDE BY SIDE

Truth be told, we really only know what works for ourselves. It would be arrogant of me to think that I know what's best for someone else. How could I? I might think that I know, and I might act like I know; but I've never traveled their path. I've never walked in their shoes. I'm not them in that moment needing to get that particular lesson from that particular situation. I can share with them about things that have carried me through my life's trials, but I can't honestly know what's best for them or what they need to do for themselves. For this reason, I now mind my own business. Instead of standing above people, thinking I know best, I now choose to stand beside them. From this position, I'm no longer hindering them from realizing their own greatness and capabilities. As a coach, I guide people into discovering their own direction rather than telling them what they should or shouldn't do. In guiding, I get to relish witnessing others discover the luminosity within themselves.

As our arrogance subsides, so does the codependent nature of our relationships. Instead of unintentionally sending the message to others that they need us, we send them the message that they are perfectly capable of piloting their lives on their own. They're now liberated to meet their own needs and depend upon themselves. Standing tall in their competence, they see how self-reliant they are. This allots them the euphoria of rising and expanding beyond their wildest imagination. Our only role is to walk beside people in support instead of doing it for them or telling them how. We greatly empower other people by allowing them ownership of their own journey.

13

NEW TRUTHS, NEW WORLD

As you continue to discover new ways of being that endow you with the power to transform your reality, your current perception of the world will factor in significantly. It will become important for you to identify the ideas and beliefs that you hold to be true. Now, I'm not talking about actual facts like the law of gravity or the price of gas. I'm referring to the beliefs that you hold that limit you, separate you from others, create adversaries, and that cause you pain or hardship. I'm talking about beliefs that disempower you. Again, *these are the concepts and convictions that your frightened mind considers to be definitive.* They are the axioms that you tell yourself are black and white, cut and dried, or undebatable.

I often hear similar themes from many of my clients. Perhaps some of them are included in your repertoire. Place a check mark next to those that apply to you, and feel free to add your own, as well.

- [ ] *I'm not good enough.*
- [ ] *It's always my fault.*
- [ ] *There is something wrong with me.*
- [ ] *I don't have enough money.*
- [ ] *I don't fit in.*
- [ ] *I'm stupid.*
- [ ] *It's not fair.*
- [ ] *It's because of you.*
- [ ] *You can't trust people.*
- [ ] *I'm too tired.*
- [ ] *I don't have enough time.*
- [ ] *People are only out for themselves.*
- [ ] *It's too late.*
- [ ] *The other shoe always drops.*
- [ ] *I'm always set up to fail.*
- [ ] *People are cruel.*
- [ ] *Life is hard.*
- [ ] *I should be making better use of my time.*
- [ ] *I deserve to be punished.*
- [ ] *I'm not motivated.*
- [ ] *I'm a bad _____.*
- [ ] *What I say doesn't matter.*

- ☐ *I'm not skinny enough.*
- ☐ *I have to work hard.*
- ☐ *I'm not interesting.*
- ☐ *I'm not sexy.*
- ☐ *I'm a burden.*
- ☐ *I'm to be ashamed of.*
- ☐ *My best is never good enough.*
- ☐ *I can't do it.*
- ☐ *I'm too old.*
- ☐ *I don't deserve it; I haven't earned it.*
- ☐ *You are my responsibility.*
- ☐ *Change is hard.*

Think about those axioms that you live by as though they were fact. Notice whether you feel empowered by them or disempowered by them, because these beliefs are the thoughts that are shaping your world right now. If you look at the specific themes on your own list and then look at your life, you will surely see how your world is a direct reflection of what you believe to be true. Your limiting tenets keep you in bondage to them and to your frightened mind. They will determine what you can and cannot do and what you will and will not do. Subscribing to them revokes your power and puts you at their mercy, as they are now calling the shots. Know that these beliefs have the ability not only to consume you, but also to make you completely dependent and reliant upon them. They're relentless. While you are under their spell, they will dominate and dictate your behavior, feelings, and actions. The amount of time and energy that you will devote to proving their rightness is beyond absurd. Can you see how these beliefs are using you and limiting your life? You no longer need to serve as their host.

It is vital that you become aware of the beliefs that you've been hosting. This awareness alone will allow you a minute amount of space between you and your limiting beliefs. In time, this space will begin to grow until you can distinguish between which thoughts are spawned from your authentic self and which thoughts are spawned from your frightened mind. This means that, as you grow in consciousness, you'll get to one day decide which thoughts you'd like to keep and of which thoughts you'd like to dispose. Giving voice to our beliefs will eventually allow us to be emancipated from them. It is important that we venture inside of them and do the work necessary to be released from their constraints. This excavation will serve you greatly.

> Please give yourself a moment to jot down some of the beliefs that prevent you from living a life of fulfillment. Next, ask yourself the questions from Chapter 9: *How does adhering to this belief serve me? What do I get out of subscribing to it? What is my reward for housing it? What is my payoff for harboring it? Does this tenet*

limit or liberate me? In addition, you might also want to ask yourself:

- *How am I protected by adhering to this belief?*
- *What am I hiding, avoiding, or putting off doing by consuming myself in this belief?*
- *What behavior does agreeing with this belief authorize me to exhibit? Is this behavior harming me or benefitting me? If it is harming me, what do I need to do about it?*
- *Does having this belief bring me peace, or does it cause me stress?*
- *How do I use this belief as an excuse for my actions?*
- *What would my life be like as a result of no longer living in concurrence with this belief?*

In this self-examination, we never know what will be revealed. For this reason, please surround yourself with as much support as you can. Lifelines are a crucial and excellent resource. It is important that we remember to keep them close, to reach out to them, and to utilize them. Giving others the opportunity to support us is a huge gift that we give to them. Please choose the lifelines that best take care of you, that feel safe, and that bring you the most nourishment. Perhaps you have meetings, a parish, or organized support groups that you attend. Maybe it's a close friend, coach, sponsor, mentor, or a counselor. Your lifelines might also include prayer, meditation, or journaling. Whatever they may be, please give yourself the permission to call upon your lifelines for support.

One of my favorite lifelines is journaling. I find the experience to be highly effective and deeply profound. It's very cathartic for me to get to be with myself, my feelings, and my thoughts. It's cleansing to let everything flow out of me without censorship. Journaling allows me a forum to express my burdens, triumphs, experiences, and concerns. It gives me a place to unload any woes. This avenue of expression is transformative. It allows me the benefit of getting my thoughts in line and on the page so that I can have a clearer understanding of what is happening within me at any given moment. It pulls me out of the cyclical hamster wheel that is my mind when I keep circulating and recycling the same chastisement. Journaling right into and through what we're believing and feeling gives our struggle an outlet to be released so that it no longer gnaws at our insides and impedes our lives. In the absence of mental clutter, a clarity reveals itself whereby our perceptions shift, our perspective broadens, and we can see through eyes of love again. That clarity leaves us more creative, more resourceful, and unstoppable.

Initiate your own healing. Please pause and give yourself a moment to journal into any struggle, concern, or even confusion that you might be experiencing right now.

Enjoy the host of new truths that awaits you as you awaken and grow in consciousness:

- *I am beautiful exactly as I am.*
- *I am desirable.*
- *I am easy to love.*
- *My voice matters.*
- *I am deserving.*
- *I am surrounded by love.*
- *Life supports me.*
- *I am rich in every way.*
- *People are generous and helpful.*
- *I am a magnet for all that is good.*
- *I am safe.*
- *All is as it should be.*
- *It always works out.*
- *I can.*
- *I treat myself with respect.*
- *I am fearless.*
- *I'm always provided for.*
- *My life is filled with joy.*
- *I express myself with ease.*
- *I wholeheartedly approve of me.*
- *I'm a delight to be around.*
- *I am good to myself.*
- *I'm genuinely happy for others' success.*
- *My work is a joy and a pleasure.*
- *Meaningful, lucrative opportunities present themselves to me daily.*
- *I am happy with my life.*

- *I trust.*
- *I welcome change.*
- *I am guilt-free.*
- *I don't ever have to compromise my integrity.*
- *Life is easy.*
- *I'm just getting started.*

14

THE WAY THROUGH

Much of society takes it as given that we live in a vertical world. Let me explain what I mean by this. When we're disconnected from our higher selves, our frightened mind will run amok, trumping up scenarios that pit us against ourselves; that pit us against others; and that tell us that we're not good enough. It will portray some people as above us and others as below us on an imaginary vertical scale that measures our value and worth. This hierarchy is contrived in order to make sense of our world so that we know where and how we fit into it and where and how others fit into it. When you think about it, it's really a lose-lose for all involved. Our frightened mind will perceive our peer whose income is twice that of ours as above us, for instance, because she earns more money than we do. Whereas, the busboy at the restaurant is somewhere lower on the hierarchy, because he's waiting on us. Many people put celebrities on a pedestal of superior rank and view human beings living on the street as second-class citizens. Can you see how our unconsciousness is creating segregation, opposition, and division on our planet? How many of you rank yourselves lower than the leader of your congregation, because you feel that he's morally superior to you? We can never measure up or be enough within the dynamic of a vertical hierarchy, because our frightened minds will always tell us that there are people who are above us. Nor is there room for any unity or oneness when we're consistently positioning others as below us.

Many of us share the belief that we're not enough as we are. Let's just admit it and put it out there. We're incessantly terrified of others finding out how we actually feel about ourselves and where we believe our place is on that vertical hierarchy. In order to disguise our fear and prevent our rank from being exposed, our frightened minds cleverly contrive personas that we hope will throw others off the scent. These characters are simply portrayals; please do not confuse them with the truth of who you are. As you know, when we inhabit such fraudulent personas, there is no room to just be, as we're consumed by the charade and the possibility of being exposed. Our lives get reduced to managing and presenting these images.

Our false identities are just ruses that we use to get by in life. They are simply fabrications that we think solidify our function and our position in the world. We feel safe in knowing how to operate within these confines, because it's so familiar to us. However, they limit our world and what's possible for us in our lives. They keep us miles away from our authentic selves. How much longer do you want to just get by?

False identities come in many personas and serve various functions. For example, false identities:

- get you what you want;
- get you what you think you need;
- limit you (because, while under their rule, you have to adhere to them);
- keep you feeling separate, different, and misunderstood;
- keep you feeling safe, protected, and on the periphery;
- are used to keep others in your life, liking you;
- are used as a method of fitting in or belonging;
- are used to gain approval, attention, applause, or to win over others;
- feel obligatory;
- keep you feeling superior and slightly elevated;
- keep you small and feeling inferior;
- keep you from the awareness of your greatness;
- keep you from the cognizance of your higher self; and
- are not who you are, even though you might be very good at inhabiting them.

Please take note of how you talk about yourself, refer to yourself, label yourself, and introduce yourself. This will provide you with the clues necessary for you to identify the false identities that you might be hosting. There are an infinite number of false identities. I've provided some examples below to get you thinking. Place a check mark next to those you've inhabited:

- [ ] the know-it-all
- [ ] the shy one
- [ ] the perfectionist
- [ ] the organizer
- [ ] the performer
- [ ] the helper
- [ ] the peacemaker
- [ ] the problem child
- [ ] the dumb one
- [ ] the flirt
- [ ] the caretaker
- [ ] the enabler
- [ ] the rebel
- [ ] the selfish one
- [ ] the giver
- [ ] the undeserving one
- [ ] the unworthy one
- [ ] the worthless one
- [ ] the nice one
- [ ] the sacrificer

- [ ] the enlightened one
- [ ] the burden
- [ ] the defective, broken one
- [ ] the outcast
- [ ] the misfit
- [ ] the pretty one
- [ ] the handsome one
- [ ] the sexy one
- [ ] the addict
- [ ] the intellectual
- [ ] the smart one
- [ ] the crazy one
- [ ] the victim
- [ ] the problem solver
- [ ] the therapist
- [ ] the disappointment
- [ ] the funny one
- [ ] the fitness fanatic
- [ ] the angry one
- [ ] the disrespected one
- [ ] the unappreciated one
- [ ] the chameleon
- [ ] the dispensable one
- [ ] the abused one
- [ ] the neglected one
- [ ] the abandoned one
- [ ] the black sheep

- [ ] the damaged goods
- [ ] the good _____
- [ ] the bad _____
- [ ] the fat one
- [ ] the positive one
- [ ] the negative one
- [ ] the confused one
- [ ] the sick one
- [ ] the "free spirit"
- [ ] the appropriate one
- [ ] the inappropriate one
- [ ] the sweet one
- [ ] the worrier
- [ ] the cynic
- [ ] the entitled one
- [ ] the unentitled one
- [ ] the weird one
- [ ] the generous one
- [ ] the poor one
- [ ] the provider
- [ ] the controller
- [ ] the supporter
- [ ] the analyzer
- [ ] the loving one
- [ ] the understanding one
- [ ] the undesired one
- [ ] the widow/widower

- ☐ the star
- ☐ the strong one
- ☐ the screw-up
- ☐ the failure
- ☐ the loser
- ☐ the patient one
- ☐ the impatient one
- ☐ the kind one
- ☐ the mean one
- ☐ the do-gooder
- ☐ the rock
- ☐ the one who's always right
- ☐ the wounded one
- ☐ the loyal one
- ☐ the people pleaser
- ☐ the skeptic
- ☐ the doormat
- ☐ the absent-minded one
- ☐ the troublemaker
- ☐ the favorite

If you find that you've attached yourself to any other personas, identities, or labels, please feel free to add them to the list, for the recognition alone will begin to relieve you from their servitude. That awareness will begin to jostle them loose and create some space between you and them.

As you grow more alert, you'll be able to recognize whether you're operating from your authentic self or operating out of a false identity. You'll be able to feel the difference. It will be very noticeable. One will feel simple and effortless, the other taxing and hard. If you find yourself keeping score, turning someone or something into an enemy, policing those around you, thinking that you know what's best for someone else, or judging yourself or others, you can rest assured that you're inhabiting a false identity. If you find yourself in opposition to anyone or anything, or if you're feeling unappreciated, disrespected, or victimized in any way, you guessed it – you're bound by a false identity. Whenever something feels personal in general, it's a clear indicator of a hit to our ego, which means that we're immersed in one of our personas. As we become aware of what does and does not feel kind and respectful to ourselves, we cease employing our false identities as a way to get by. It becomes too dishonest, stressful, and painful to abdicate our truth and integrity to embody a character.

When we're under the influence of our false identities, we are neither present nor available. Others may enjoy our false identity, but our authentic self is locked away and inaccessible. Is it any wonder, then, when we feel a lack of closeness or connection in our lives?

The beauty of our false identities is that each one can guide us directly into new ways of being, higher levels of consciousness, and our divine nature. In order for this to occur, we must have faith that our feelings can bring us deeper levels of healing, understanding, and awareness. It is important, throughout this journey, to hold fast to the knowledge that all of our feelings were created to bring us back home to ourselves. They are not intended to punish or torment us, but rather to assist and direct us. Feelings point us in the direction in which our souls are inspired to move. They are always happening for our greater good and for our expansion and evolution. All of my feelings have been my university and have served as the tarmac for my ascension. As I have surrendered into embracing them, they have always brought me to higher ground.

Below is an exercise that will allow you to experience for yourself the journey from false identity to liberation. It is essential to be willing and open and to trust this process.

1. Name one of your false identities.
2. List any disempowering beliefs and limiting mantras that you have as a result of adhering to that identity.
3. List the feelings that spawn from those disempowering beliefs and mantras.
4. When these feelings come up for you, give yourself the permission to acknowledge and to experience each one. Then, enjoy the new states of being that emerge as each feeling loses its charge.

Here's how this fourth step works: as we know,

leaning into and embracing our feelings allows them to begin to slip away. I'm not saying that you have to take them on permanently. I'm just asking that you please allow yourself to fully experience them, to open yourself up to them so that they may begin to lose their grip on you. As they do, notice what happens inside of you. Notice how much freer you feel; how much deeper you breathe; how much taller you stand. Notice how much space you have created for yourself. Notice how it feels inside of you. Notice the qualities, characteristics, and new states of being that emerge and rise up within you. Notice how much more centered and empowered you feel. Notice how it feels to be you. Acknowledging and welcoming each feeling allows you to witness where it's carrying you. *In delving so deeply, please remember that these feelings are not permanent; they are only temporary. However, they will hang around longer if you are in resistance to them. For your benefit, please maintain access to your lifelines.*

Allow me to give you an example.

1. One popular false identity is that of "the Victim".
2. Someone who identifies as the Victim might have some of the following disempowering beliefs and limiting mantras:
    A. *People take advantage of me.*
    B. *You made me feel this way.*
    C. *They're just using me.*

D. *You take me for granted.*

E. *It's your fault.*

F. *If it wasn't for _____, I could _____.*

In each step, the examples listed as A-F correspond with the same letters (A-F) for the following steps. For example, the belief listed after "A" in Step 2 spawns the feelings listed after "A" in Step 3.

3. Some of the feelings that spawn from each of the above beliefs likely include:

     A. resentment, anger, <u>irritation</u>

     B. helplessness, <u>hurt</u>, hostility

     C. <u>betrayal</u>, disrespected, rage

     D. <u>undervalued</u>, unappreciated, dissatisfied

     E. aggravated, frustrated, <u>vengeful</u>

     F. hopelessness, disappointment, <u>despair</u>

4. Here are some of the new feelings and states of being that could emerge as one embraces the feelings associated with each of the beliefs or mantras. *Examples are in reference to the underlined feeling in the corresponding letter above.*

     A. clarity; serenity

     B. loving; empathy

     C. forgiveness; revitalization

     D. confidence; dignity

     E. unburdened; accessible

     F. emancipation; inspiration

In this exploration, we come to realize that all of our feelings just want to be accepted (and not rejected) by us. They're awaiting our recognition. When we are ready to answer our feelings' plea for attention, we can embrace them and even celebrate them for where they're taking us – to higher ground. We get to love and understand them.

As we make peace with all that is happening inside of us, we get to live in harmony with all that is. Our once vertical hierarchy begins to morph into a horizontal world of unity where we are no longer at odds with ourselves nor are we competing with or threatened by others. We're genuinely happy and excited for other people's triumphs and successes. In this untiered world, we no longer perceive anyone or anything as being above us, below us, or against us. Everyone and everything aligns beside us in support of us on this even playing field of equality.

In this journey of awakening and becoming more mindful, you'll come to comprehend that you are not your false identity behavior. Nor are you your thoughts or your feelings. There is a self-emancipation that comes when we see and know that our thoughts are just thoughts and that our feelings are just feelings: they don't define us, and they are certainly not accurate representations of who we are. There is a vast difference between the truth of who we are and what is currently happening inside of us at any given moment. Remember, pay attention to what you're thinking and notice how you feel when you're thinking it. If you're unsure as to what you're thinking, pay attention to your feelings. Your feelings will always lead back to what you're currently thinking. They will illuminate what it is that you're believing to be true in that moment. Then, pay attention to the type of behavior that you exhibit as a result of those feelings. To take it one step further, ask yourself: *Is this behavior in alignment with the person I'd like to be? Does this behavior support the person I'd like to become?*

15

THE BEST POLICY

Honest communication can significantly simplify and enhance the way we experience life as a whole. By "honest communication", I'm talking about first being honest with ourselves in regard to what does or doesn't feel right for us and then allowing our self-honesty to transcend into our relationships. Our first loyalty is to ourselves and our well-being. For this reason, I encourage my clients to always be loyal to their own voice and to their own truth first. By staying true to ourselves, our feelings, and our values, we cultivate personal integrity. That personal integrity provides us with a self-reliant foundation from which to communicate.

Staying true to ourselves ensures that we are free to communicate openly, honestly, and directly. Staying loyal to ourselves means that we can no longer force ourselves to act out of duty or obligation to others. We come to understand that our only obligation is to ourselves and our integrity. Regardless of the way that others might respond, we are allowed to act on what is true for us. We are never obligated to say *yes* to someone, when we really mean *no*. We may not always be the most popular person in the room, but I promise you, the rewards are immense. Acting from truthfulness and authenticity, we have everything to gain. By staying loyal and true to us, we finally get ourselves back: confidence, self-esteem, and all. There's nothing like being able to count on yourself one hundred percent of the time.

Communicating honestly doesn't mean that we get to assault others with our words under the guise of "just being honest". No, we are always responsible for what we say, our delivery, and any reactions we might have to someone else's response. In addition, consider your intention for each exchange. Are you wanting to bridge a gap? Do you want to feel closer to someone? Do you want to establish more trust in the relationship? Know your intention. You might want to state it, as well, should it feel organic for you to do so.

In my own honest communication, I have found that when I'm being loving and kind, my honesty is received with willingness and appreciation. However, when there is righteousness or shaming in my tone, my words are usually met with defensiveness and argument. From moment to moment I notice any reaction that my delivery might be evoking. This reveals any position that I might be taking and allows me to shift to a more neutral stance. We are always responsible for the way we participate in our inter-actions. Are you being open, unbiased, and receptive, where dialogue and conversation safely flow between the two of you? Or, are you positioned in authority, where you find yourself lecturing, enlightening, or blaming? One unites, rectifies, and amends, where the other alienates, divides, and renders the other person wrong. Decide for yourself how you want your relationships to be.

16

Transparency

I have no doubt that we've all had times where we've found ourselves feeling frustrated, angry, or resentful, because we aren't getting what we want. We believe that we have effectively stated what we want. We believe that we have made a clear request, and it isn't being fulfilled. That may be true. However, sometimes we think we're communicating effectively, when instead we're testing, challenging, hinting, manipulating through emotion, assuming someone should just know, or speaking in code. Though we think that we've made our point, have we really? Can you honestly say that your communication was clear, clean, and direct? There's no need to perpetuate more hurt, disappointment, or heartache for yourself. Please take notice of (and accountability for) all your transmissions. We cannot assume that other people are telepathic. They can't decipher what it is that we want or expect if we're not directly stating it.

Can you just come right out and clearly state your requests? Can you allow yourself the permission to be open and vulnerable without any uncleanliness? Instead of saying, "I hate going to my company parties alone," for example, perhaps you could say, "I'd love it if you would join me for my company barbeque this Saturday." This way, the other person will have an accurate idea of what it is that you want, and they will know whether they are willing or able to give it to you. Another's compliance (or noncompliance) is simply a reflection of whether he or she can honor our request, period. Neither decision has anything to do with us. They can either do it, or they can't. There is no hidden meaning. We're the ones who assign meaning when someone does or doesn't do what we wanted them to do. By doing so, we clog the flow in our relationships. Pay attention to the significance that you attach to what others do or don't do for you. What if you are not correct? When we take others' actions personally, it's because we think we need something from them in that moment. We often want them to validate or invalidate something we believe to be true about ourselves. So in essence, we're using them to prove something to ourselves. Instead of wanting them to do what's true for them, we want them to accommodate us.

Wouldn't you prefer that we all stay true to ourselves, as challenging as that might be at times? When there is no longer meaning associated with the granting or denying of requests, our relationships become so much simpler, safer, and more intimate. It's amazing what transpires. We stop feeling the need to meet others' requests in order to prove that we love, care about, value, or respect them. In turn, they are no longer required to meet our requests to prove the same to us: that they love, care about, value, or respect us or, more important, that we *are worth* loving, caring about, valuing, or respecting. We don't need to use others to evaluate our worth. We are perfect and enough exactly as we are. Dare to be enough as you are and to be clean in all of your exchanges.

17

Express Yourself

For the majority of my years, I lived by the mantra: *Tell me who you want me to be so that I can be that; please don't discard me and throw me away.* It's clear that, in my desperation, I didn't have a strong sense of myself, nor did I know that I had any value. I would abandon myself and my needs at all costs to do my best to make you happy, to keep you in my life, and to keep you from seeing (and me from feeling) the shame, self-loathing, hurt, and emptiness that was churning inside of me. I'd say "Yes" when I meant yes. I'd say "Yes" when I meant no. I'd say "Yes" when I meant *not on your life.* Living in that fraudulence was terrifying, as I lost more of myself every day. I just didn't know that I was worthy enough to be honest. I thought that I had to tell people what I thought they wanted to hear so that things wouldn't change between us and so they would never leave.

The thought of being alone with myself was haunting, and I was bound to not let that happen.

Through my self-actualization work, I realized that my inability to say no had been centered around so much fear – I mean *so* much fear. As I grew more honest with myself, it became very evident how much that fear had been running my life. I was deathly afraid of being seen as anything other than a nice and kind person. I knew how to operate and function within this persona, as I had spent decades creating and mastering it to perfection. I had constructed it in the first place to avoid being perceived as selfish and ultimately disappointing, upsetting, or hurting someone. I never learned how to be kind and honest at the same time. In the home where I grew up, words like "no" were shouted in varying degrees of shameful reprimand to wound and to win. So I found it very difficult to trust that I wouldn't offend by being honest. I was terrified of rejection, of being dispensable, of not being liked, and of losing love, affection, or approval. It was a painful way to get by. But my biggest fear was claiming and stepping into my power. You see, my ability to say no and to be honest would have undermined the persona I was presenting and contradicted how I felt about myself. Saying no would have meant that I have value, that my voice matters, that I'm enough, and that I'm deserving of goodness, kindness, and decency.

My life has shifted a great deal now that I understand the value and the rewards of being honest. I find it imperative to my well-being that I be truthful and fully self-expressed. I no longer compromise my magnificence by making myself smaller or dimming my light to keep people in my life. I do my best to always stay true to me and to face any fears as they arise. My confidence and self-esteem have increased as I've learned to keep my yeses honest and my nos honest, because I can finally rely on me to be truthful. I've replaced explaining, rationalizing, or attempting to convince or change the mind of another with tools like: *that doesn't work for me, that doesn't feel appropriate for me, that's not okay with me, I'm not comfortable with that*, and simply *no, thank you*. There is an enormous weight that gets lifted once we can say *no* without justifying or defending ourselves. At the beginning, I kept my yeses and nos honest when I could. When I was unable to do so for whatever reason, I did my best to accept the fact that I couldn't in that particular situation, and I learned from what my fraudulence had to teach me.

How self-expressed are you? How truthful and honest are you with yourself and with others? Let's put it to the test. See if you can be completely honest for a 24-hour period. This is no small task, I promise you. This is an opportunity for you to get to see where you stand for yourself and where you don't. It will be very beneficial for you to pay attention to what inner commentaries, feelings, behaviors, and reactions arise for you in this 24-hour period. Notice what happens within your body, what you're feeling. What do you feel compelled to say? What is it that you wish that you could say? What do you *not* feel the need to say? This is just about you observing you. Notice if you're being guided by your heart or led by your frightened mind. Use this time to really see what feels okay with you, what doesn't feel okay with you, what works for you, what doesn't work for you.

In this awakening, what now feels appropriate? What doesn't? Consider what best takes care of you and what you need to do for yourself. Do your best to stay true to you. As we become more authentic, we find ourselves more present to enjoy our experiences. In our full self-expression, when something doesn't work for us, we can clearly, lovingly, and simply say so without feeling that we need to explain ourselves, offer up anything, or feel guilty. You're enough to say no. Please remember, a *no* from your heart is a *yes* to your life.

18

To Me, From Me

Whatever it is that you believe you need from another, try giving it to yourself. See if that doesn't shift not only your perspective, but also the dynamic of the relationship, your level of satisfaction, and your life as a whole. When we place responsibility for our happiness and gratification upon another human being, we create unnecessary pain and suffering for ourselves. Whenever we believe that someone else should fill our emotional needs and provide us with love, understanding, value, appreciation, or whatever it is that we want, we set ourselves up for a world of hurt. I'm human. I get it. I really do. I understand how nice it feels when someone's being loving, kind, attentive, or affectionate with me. I get how comforting that can be. I'm just saying that it's *my* job (not someone else's) to *be* those things and to give those things to myself. This way, when someone bestows me with affection, I'm simply grateful for their outpouring of kindness and generosity. Giving to myself what I thought I needed from you keeps my relationships clean and without condition.

Let me ask you something: do you feel worthy and deserving of goodness, kindness, and decency? If you don't, then others' affections will never suffice. They will never be enough or look the way you think they should. We can only accept from others what our internal monologues mandate. This is why, when someone tells you they love you, you might have a challenging time receiving or believing it. If you don't even believe that you're worthy of it, you're going to have a difficult time letting it in. Whatever you think you need from another, can you please begin to accept that from yourself? There is no other person whom you need to love, understand, value, or appreciate you. It's your right and responsibility to be that for yourself. When we give to ourselves what we think we need from another, we witness an immense shift in our perceptions and, therefore, in our relationships and our lives.

What are the ways that you can be more generous and nurturing with you? There are many ways for you to foster this discovery. I begin every day by giving the first hour or so to myself. This means no cell phones, no emails, no phone calls – nothing. I spend this time nourishing myself with prayer, affirmations, and meditation. This ritual grounds me, sources me, and centers me. It's a tranquil way to enter each day. I also gift myself with sacred moments of hiking in nature or surrendering my being in a yoga class. Cleansing myself in this manner ensures a sharper clarity throughout my day. I show myself appreciation by choosing the best foods for my body, by getting sufficient rest, and by treating myself to cranial-sacral massage. By being truthful, having integrity, and taking accountability for my life, I show myself respect. In addition, I find it to be incredibly loving with me to ask for help, to delegate, and to have set work hours. Finally, maintaining a constant connection with God is where I receive the most nourishment. In the presence of that relationship, I don't feel the need to seek anything from anyone: not my parents, not my friends, not even my spouse. In that alliance, I'm full, present, completely taken care of, and the best me possible. I invite you to find and foster what nourishes you and begin to implement that into your life. You'll be grateful that you did. It is by serving yourself that you serve others. It is by serving yourself that you serve the world.

19

As It Is

Being in opposition to our current reality will guarantee our suffering and likely affect those who surround us. Such distress is caused by our unwillingness to allow ourselves to just have what we have and to allow each moment to be as it is. Now, I'm not saying that life doesn't bring us challenges that are difficult to endure. I'm just saying that we bring on greater suffering for ourselves when we think that it shouldn't be happening the way that it is. By thinking that our current circumstance should be different than it is, we exacerbate our misery. Let me explain. Let's say that you come from a family where there's a clear difference between how the siblings are treated. Half of your siblings are lavished with time, attention, and niceties, while the other half are not. So from your perspective, it seems like half of you are favored where the other half aren't. Now, would it be the variation in the treatment of the siblings that might cause you stress, or is it your belief that all of you should be treated equally that could cause you suffering? In addition, would your beliefs about what's fair and not fair and what's appropriate and not appropriate also factor into this matter?

Whenever we are in resistance to what is, in opposition to what is before us, it's the ensuing thoughts and commentary that amplify our stressful feelings. So when you feel tension in your body, pause for a moment and see if you can identify and isolate the thought that is prompting you to feel that way. The stress you feel is your indicator that the thought perpetuating it is opposing your reality and therefore requires your attention and excavation. If we can accept the entirety of the situation, and I understand what an undertaking this can be at times, we will not be consumed by the added agitation that comes from arguing with what is. Accepting the situation at hand allows us the clarity to know how to function and proceed in the way that best takes care of us. This enables us to remain present and even calm in situations that once triggered us. Now, accepting what is before us doesn't require us to like it, agree with it, or condone it. At the same time, we are not passive, resigned, or turning a blind eye, either. In the acceptance of what is, we give our lives and sanity back to ourselves and forgo any additional suffering in regard to that situation.

How do you know that whatever is currently happening is exactly as it should be? Because it is. That's just the deal. How do you know that you're exactly where you're supposed to be? Because you are. It's pretty much that simple. It couldn't be any other way based upon what is evident in this exact moment. Should you like to dispute this, just refer to the moment at hand. The facts of the present moment are always accurate, one hundred percent of the time.

20

HEAD-ON

Acceptance, for me, is a declaration of movement. For you see, in the *acceptance of what is,* we open and become accessible. This means that our minds open and our hearts open, not only to ourselves, but also to our current situation as a whole. This favorable reception creates space inside of us. Within that space exists a sanctuary of calm that enables us to connect with our divine intuition. That inner sanctuary hosts the most sacred peace for which many of us have been longing. Within that peace resides the clarity to guide our footsteps. Living in clear and peaceful presence, we are still and available to receive the divine guidance for creating our lives, knowing what inspired action to take, and determining what to do in any given situation.

For me, acceptance paves the road to freedom. It's a wonderful existence to be sourced by my higher self instead of my frightened mind. When we cease arguing with our current circumstance, we have the ability to put our full energy toward whatever our heart desires. By accepting and facing what is standing before us, we have a solid foundation upon which to stand and to build, from which to move, to heal, and to grow. I find it highly beneficial to my well-being to lay out the welcome mat for whatever is before me. This means that I bring it in closer to learn from what it has to teach me, which avails me of the higher ground where I am being taken.

As we now know, by accepting the totality of a situation, we create more spaciousness inside of ourselves. In that space is a blissful, still, calm through which we connect to our source and our higher selves. This enables us to receive the most supreme guidance. Now, if you are finding it difficult to accept the totality of the situation at hand, just take in a few long, deep breaths and see if you can accept the fact that you're not ready to accept it yet. Either way is okay, I promise. We're ready when we're ready. By accepting that we're not able or ready to accept what is happening, we are still awakening and, thus, still creating that internal space for healing and movement.

21

THE HUSTLE

When we lose the awareness of our true selves, our frightened minds take over, and the focus shifts to the preservation of our false identities. For this reason, I would like you to really pay attention to the "dances" that your false identities orchestrate. Now, when I say "dances", what I'm referring to are the methods by which our false identities maneuver through life in order to get us what we want. They are an artful mode of self-preservation, a masterful way to carry on and persevere instead of giving up in the face of fear. Our dances are fashioned out of the masks we wear, the things we say, the things we do, and the costumes we don to support our false identities – our inauthentic representations. We wear these masks for various reasons: from concealing, camouflaging, and protecting our hearts to veneering the unworthiness, fear, shame, and inadequacy that often reside within us.

The moment we believe that our false identities are who we are, we lose touch with our inner sanctuary of calm. In our confusion, we become discontent. As our restlessness amplifies and intensifies, we find our dances gaining momentum. We begin dancing as fast as we can and as far away from the cognizance of our true selves as possible. For me, feeling lost and separate from my true self prompted my frightened mind to kick in and work overtime at being the over-generous, over-accessible, over-kind person (a.k.a., the "people pleaser"). That false identity mandated my every move and tirelessly dictated my dance. Keeping up this persona was exhausting. I would stay on the phone with you until 4 a.m., console you, never say no, rearrange my schedule to accommodate you, pay for most of our outings together, discount my services, and do pretty much whatever you wanted me to do. I would give you as much of me as I could to keep you around, to keep you satisfied, and to keep me from having to be alone with myself. I gave you more of me than I ever gave to myself. I just didn't know any better. I spent countless, precious moments trying to control how you felt about me so that you would never see the chaos, turbulence, and emptiness I felt inside. I never wanted you to know how shitty I felt about myself and how unworthy I felt of your friendship.

Continue to learn with each passing moment, especially in regard to the confining effects your dances have upon your life:

- Pay attention to the dances that your false identities create.
- What are you looking for in each dance?
- What do you hope to get from it? What do you actually get out of doing it?
- What prompts your dance? What are its steps?
- Notice what you're trying to avoid by implementing your dance.
- Notice your internal monologue both while in your dance and in its aftermath.
- Notice the feelings that accompany your internal monologue.
- Notice how it feels to be you within your dance, and, notice what happens to your self-trust, your confidence, and your belief in yourself as a result of your dance.
- Ask yourself what your dances cause you to miss out on.
- Ask yourself what your dances cost you.
- What do you fear you will lose without having your dance to shield you?

The more that you notice how unkind it feels within you to adhere to your dances, the more difficult it becomes to live with their effects. As you ascend in consciousness, you will become unable to treat yourself disrespectfully in that way. Once it's no longer an option to be dishonest or inauthentic, we find that our dances start to lose their momentum.

22

CHECK IN

As you become more conscious of your dances and your false identities, you will likely find it arduous to go on fabricating personas or dancing, even when you might be inclined to do so. The places in your life where you are fearful, taking the easy way out, being fraudulent, or not living in alignment with your truth become clearer and more evident. With this newfound awareness, inhabiting and perpetuating your dances will no longer seem as natural as it once did. Nor will it work for you in the same way it once did. That behavior will likely become an integrity issue for you as you awaken, become more truthful and honest, and align with your authentic self.

Below are examples of some behaviors, concepts, and ways of being that you might find to now be out of alignment with your integrity. These examples are simply barometers for you to gauge where you are along your path of self-actualization. Many of these may be works in progress for you. Please honor your place in your journey, and be gentle with yourself as you peruse this list. Which of the following might now be out of line with your integrity? Place a check mark next to any that apply.

☐ Dancing
☐ Overcompensating
☐ Apologizing for being you
☐ Not standing up for yourself
☐ Not being true to yourself and your feelings
☐ Resisting what is
☐ Stifling your voice
☐ Believing that you deserve to be punished
☐ Not complying with your own boundaries
☐ Being dishonest
☐ Enabling codependency in your relationships
☐ Consistently eating unhealthfully
☐ Neglecting to get ample exercise
☐ Making yourself smaller to accommodate others
☐ Saying yes when you want to say no
☐ Lashing out
☐ Habitually being late

- [ ] Saying what you think someone wants to hear or what sounds good
- [ ] Not keeping your relationships, exchanges, and interactions clean
- [ ] People pleasing
- [ ] Seeking validation
- [ ] Believing that you are not enough as you are
- [ ] Living irresponsibly
- [ ] Looking outside of yourself to fill you
- [ ] Not trusting your instincts
- [ ] Attempting to control other people or situations
- [ ] Passive-aggressive behavior
- [ ] Burying yourself in material wants
- [ ] Selling yourself short
- [ ] Immersing yourself in distractions to avoid being with yourself and your thoughts
- [ ] Reacting in righteous defense
- [ ] Holding on to grudges and resentments
- [ ] Believing that you are a bother to people
- [ ] Being harsh or critical with yourself
- [ ] Not being forgiving or merciful with yourself
- [ ] Believing that there's something wrong with you
- [ ] Not keeping your word, especially to you
- [ ] Identifying yourself with what you have or what you do
- [ ] Living beyond your means
- [ ] Addictive behavior

☐ Gossiping

☐ Not making time for yourself

☐ Allowing your phone or computer to run your life

☐ Self-destructive behavior

☐ Not asking for help or reaching out for support or guidance

☐ Blaming others

☐ Believing that something should be different than it is

☐ Believing that someone should be different than they are

☐ Victimizing yourself by turning someone or something into an enemy

☐ Trying to fix or change another

☐ Not taking complete accountability for the totality of your life

☐ Not copping to your side of the fence (even in regard to your expectations)

☐ Comparing your life to others' lives

☐ Being unreceptive to receiving from others

☐ Not saying you're sorry or making amends

☐ Limiting yourself or boxing yourself in with labels of any nature

☐ Not adequately or lovingly caring for yourself

☐ Bullying or punishing yourself or others

☐ Not maintaining balance in your life

☐ Being unwilling, stubborn, or intransigent

☐ Not cherishing your uniqueness

☐ Not appreciating yourself or what you do
☐ Underestimating your greatness
☐ Not owning your power
☐ Not living faithfully

For me, indulging in drugs, alcohol, or anonymous sex is taking the easy way out. At this stage of my development, I feel as though I would be cheating myself. The way that I partook in drugs, alcohol, and anonymous sex was reckless and excessive. It was done in an effort to escape and seek temporary refuge from my abusive, critical thoughts and unbearable feelings. Engaging in that type of self-destructive behavior has definitely become an integrity issue for me. I no longer find it acceptable to inflict such harm upon myself.

There are countless examples of integrity issues, and they vary from person to person. The list above is to raise your level of awareness, to get you started, and to help you identify any issues that are standing in the way of you being your authentic self. These examples are also to show you how far you've come. Please give yourself the recognition you deserve. This is an ongoing process of evolution. We are forever awakening, forever growing. Can you think of other behaviors, concepts, or ways of being that might be out of line with who you know yourself to be today?

23

TRUE NORTH

Many of us have been taught that we should be the bigger person, that we should "take the high road". Doing the "right" thing out of obligation (instead of staying true to ourselves) can be accompanied by an enormous amount of anxiety, hostility, resentment, and uncertainty. For me, doing the "right" thing (when it violates my integrity) is a disservice to myself. It is dishonest. So many of us do what we feel we're supposed to do while foregoing what we know in our hearts is right for us. I understand how this can seem like the honorable route to take. However, please take a moment to consider the effect that disingenuous gestures have upon you and others.

Adhering to my integrity nullifies my impulse to try to be the bigger person or take the high road. In fact, it nullifies that concept altogether. Furthermore, it allows me the security of knowing that I can count on myself at all times to do the *honest* thing. Doing the honest thing is the right thing for me, always. I invite you to sit with that concept for a moment. How would doing the honest thing affect your life and your emotional well-being? How will trusting that the honest thing is the right thing simplify your decision-making process?

24

ALLOW

I'm confident that most of you have heard at least a few of the following phrases in your lifetime: "just be positive", "be grateful for what you have", "one day at a time", "have faith", "let it go". People often want to know what they can do to act in line with these words of wisdom. Everyone wants to know how to "let it go" or take "one day at a time", for example, when circumstances are at their toughest. However, when it comes to concepts like these, *how* is not the question. Fixating upon the *how* keeps our minds occupied with a fruitless quest. It keeps us locked in resistance, which obstructs our ability to fully accept and surrender to what is before us. It is not necessary to obsess over how to apply concepts like these. You will find it far more productive to just be present with what is. Being present will ultimately allow for those concepts to organically find a home within you.

It is possible for concepts such as these to become natural *ways of living* and *ways of being* for you. To begin, allow yourself to simply hear concepts like those above and understand them to the best of your ability. That's it. Don't fret if they don't completely sink in right away. It might take some time before they become second nature for you. That's okay. Just continue to trust the process.

I've heard and read about many concepts over the course of my life. Some of them found their place within me immediately, some took over a decade, and some are still gestating. Again, each one lands within at the exact moment that it does. I've encountered so many people who attend seminar after seminar, or who read self-help book after self-help book, desperately trying to force these concepts into their lives. They understand them intellectually and theoretically. However, in their impatience, they attempt to squeeze into the concepts as if they're trying to cram themselves into pants that are three sizes too small. It's just not possible. We can't squeeze into something that isn't a fit yet. We can't force something that's still in incubation form. These transformations happen at the exact moment that they do – not one second before, and not one second after.

I have found that the best way for these concepts to live and breathe effortlessly inside of me is to accept, surrender, and to lean into what is before me. Doing so places me into a state of allowance, where I am open and present and, thus, have access to my inner sanctuary of calm. Within that stillness, there is no forcing or fighting to separate me from those concepts. As I grow accustomed to operating from that place, concepts like "one day at a time" and "be grateful for what you have" transform from lofty slogans into inherent and authentic ways of living.

Being patient and compassionate with yourself will carry you very far. Providing acceptance and understanding for yourself through these transitions will help to light your way. Remember, it's not about forcing a concept into becoming a way of living or a way of being. Rather, it's about allowing for each to be integrated in its own, sweet time.

25

STAND BY YOU

If you're waiting for a mate, a promotion, a certain amount of money, to lose 20 pounds, for your health to improve, or for someone or something to change before you can accept your situation and enjoy your life, are you really living, or have you essentially put your happiness on hold? Here's the deal: when you don't accept the moment for what it is, you unconsciously limit that moment's possibilities. By accepting all as it is right now, you allow for the possibility of fulfillment without condition. Again, in order to accept something, you don't have to like it, agree with it, or condone it. All you need to do is open your mind to the reality of it. Here's an opportunity to do just that. In this exact moment, try allowing yourself the permission to *have what you have*: have the amount of money that you have in your bank account right now, have the job that you're in right now, have what you weigh, have your age, have your current health situation, have your level of contentment, have the state of your relationship, or have your singlehood. This would also include giving yourself permission to have the ticker tape of thoughts that runs through your mind and the resulting feelings. Remember, you don't have to buy a lifetime subscription to those feelings. All I'm asking is that you allow yourself the permission to have them when they arise.

We cannot get free from something that's lying unacknowledged and dormant inside of us. We cannot enlighten ourselves to something that we are in denial of or that we can't yet see. By simply bringing awareness to those distressing thoughts and feelings lurking within, a shift naturally begins to take place on a deep, internal level. This movement allows for our emotional underworld to dislodge, rise to the surface, and come into the light. For those of you who find it challenging to have your emotions and to be with them, I have devised a closed-eye visualization exercise that I think you will find highly beneficial. This exercise can be used for any emotion. It is one of the methods I find helpful for leaning into and making peace with my feelings. As always, be sure that you have your lifelines available, should you need their support.

> Envision yourself in your angriest moment. Close your eyes, and venture back. You might have been 6, 12, 37, or 64. Or maybe you're in that moment right now.

Pinpoint that instance. Give yourself the permission to experience it, to witness it, and to mentally go to that place, as overwhelming as it might be for you. Now, take a moment to take in the surroundings: what do you see, smell, taste, hear? Are you alone, or is someone there with you? Observe any sensations occurring in your body. Give yourself a moment to be with them. Next, notice the thoughts you're having in this moment of anger. Do any of these resonate with you? *Why are you doing this to me? You never listen. I hate you. I don't deserve this. I can't deal with this anymore.* Feel the anger accompanying those thoughts. Allow yourself to experience it to the best of your ability.

Now, let's dig deeper. What other feelings are there, dwelling beneath your anger? Perhaps you're discovering feelings of sadness. Some of you might find embarrassment, shame, loneliness, or guilt. Others might feel diminished, rejected, helpless, or trapped. Sit with these feelings for a moment, as well. Allow them to permeate your being. Again, this exercise is an invitation for any feelings lying dormant within you to rise and surface, to become your allies, and to be brought into the light. This way, you can be enlightened by them instead of being at the effect of them. There is no rush. Please take the time necessary to really surrender into this experience.

As you're sitting with these feelings, imagine that you see someone in the distance walking toward you. That person draws nearer, and you recognize them to be your higher self, the truth of who you are. Notice how they stand, how they carry themselves. Witness the light they behold. Breathe in their magnificence. As they approach, you are encompassed by a feeling of safety that's radiating from their being. Go ahead and embrace that loving being. Feel the warmth and nurturing in that envelopment. See if you can open yourself to receive that comfort and solace from your higher self in this moment of distress. Allow them to hold you, to hug you, and to nourish every part of your being. Relax, and allow that love to infuse your every cell.

Now, look into their eyes, and really see them. Connect with them. What do you notice when you peer into their eyes? Feel the synergy of love emanating within this partnership. That love is you. That love belongs to you. That love is inseparable from you. As you join hands and merge into one, allow the resounding light, joy, and beauty to beset you.

In this union, you are ever secure in your connection to your higher self. This means that you will never again have to feel lost, confused, or alone in this world, for you know that you and your higher self are one.

26

DESTINATION UNKNOWN

As humans, we will inevitably endure a multitude of trials and tribulations over the course of our lifetime. We experience legal issues, addictions, divorce, illness, loss, and so much more. Some see these events as problems, while others recognize them as challenges. As painful as they may feel, and as difficult as they may be to withstand, I truly believe that these situations are always created for our benefit. They happen for us so that we can grow in consciousness, expand, and become more mindful as human beings. These experiences provide us with some of our most profound learning. Learning, my friends, is invaluable.

Maybe you can see how *certain* challenges can be learning experiences, while you believe that others are just too trying to view in that way. That is understandable. Even though we might conceptually understand that all is occurring for our greater good, our frightened mind still chimes in (often overriding what we know is true) and tells us that this event is happening to our detriment. Because we fear the grave consequences foreseen by our frightened mind, we come to believe that we need a certain outcome to occur in order to be okay. Since it is impossible to control the outcome, our frightened mind goes into red alert. It kicks into overdrive and becomes cluttered with agitated thoughts. This makes it far more challenging for us to stay present to learn from what the situation has to teach us. Conversely, when you're not attached to a certain outcome, you're free to relish the journey, as well as the benefits, of *any* result that might occur, even if it isn't what you had in mind. When we face a situation with faith, we know that whatever the outcome may be, it is happening *for* us, regardless of whether we understand it. So when we don't get the outcome we desired, it doesn't have to be a problem anymore. Instead, we can now learn from what it has to teach us.

Let's use the term "zenagogue" to refer to the cerebral "classroom" we frequent during our especially weighty learning experiences. I'm referring to that mental space that we visit during those challenging situations from which we extract more awareness, clarity, and understanding. In order to experience the true benefit of our zenagogue, it's paramount that we be as present as we can. Again, this would entail allowing ourselves to have what we have and to be open to what is. When we find ourselves in a tough situation, we can ask ourselves: *What are my expectations in this situation? Are they creating stress or peace? How is this benefitting me right now? What am I learning? What is the lesson for me in this? What is the opportunity here?* We can notice how we're feeling, what we're thinking, and whether we're having any reactions. Our reactions alert us to what needs care, attention, and healing inside. We know that if we're having a reaction, there's an opportunity to extract a lesson (or two) from this visit to our zenagogue.

One of my zenagogue visits spanned nearly three years. In October of 1999, I was diagnosed with testicular cancer. I underwent a radical orchiectomy and the adjuvant treatments that followed. This left me up many a night, green with nausea and unable to sleep. It was during a midnight rerun of Oprah Winfrey's "Remembering Your Spirit" that I had an awakening that would shift the course and the direction of my life forever. I remember being unusually captivated by the message being conveyed in that episode. In a matter of moments, I was beset by an encompassing peace that felt safe and nurturing. Since I usually felt ill and listless at that time of night, it was a huge deal for me to be able to be so still and attentive and to feel so good. Within that peace emerged a clarity through which I was able to recognize the commencement of my life's purpose. Everything aligned at once, and it was within that stillness that I received my guidance. I was to write a book that incorporated the lessons that I'd learned from my life's experiences. I would include intimate stories so that others could relate, not feel alone in what they were going through, and ultimately be more merciful with themselves. I honored my own pace with my workload, school load, and schedule. Knowing that I could not force or rush this process, I allowed for the book to reveal itself to me and to unfold in its own perfect time. Therefore, my book took nearly five years to complete. I invented a trade name, purchased the domain for my website in September of 2002, and sent certified letters to myself regarding the use of my trade name for protection, should any legal issues arise in the future. The website sat untouched while I was in the creation of my book, for I had so much on my plate, I was still uncertain of my direction, and I wasn't yet sure of how I intended to introduce myself to the world. That revelation came to me near the end of 2005, and, thus, I filed my trademark application that December.

In March of 2006, I received a cease and desist letter from a disgruntled individual regarding my use of the trade name. Confident that I had taken enough precautions and that I'd done all the necessary footwork to ensure that there would not be an issue, I continued working to bring my vision to fruition while my trademark attorney handled the legalities. By November of 2006, I was ready to retire from hairdressing and begin my transition into full-time life coaching. I had worked diligently for the past seven years preparing for the next phase of my life by setting aside money, researching, educating myself, and working to complete my book. I had just taken that giant career leap and had even hired a high-powered public relations firm to launch my book. I was so excited for where my life was heading when, all of a sudden, I received another cease and desist letter that December. This time, however, it was from a multi-billion dollar global conglomerate claiming that my use of the trade name constituted "trademark infringement and unfair competition that is actionable in a court of law". It appeared that the individual who sent me the initial cease and desist letter had somehow become affiliated with that conglomerate. I was now involved in something far more complex than I had ever anticipated. Little did I know, my world was about to be turned upside down.

The time spent in my zenagogue throughout this process became one of the greatest learning experiences that I have ever endured. While on this rollercoaster, I did my best to yield to as many moments as I could, day by day, week by week, month by month, year by year. Yes, it was extremely costly; and yes, it grew immensely emotional at times. I can remember three-way phone calls with my lawyers where I could barely breathe, where the sobs heaved out of my body, and where I just wanted to resign and rock myself in fetal position in the corner. Those were some trying moments. I remember being so angry, feeling so devastated, and just being riddled with victimizing thoughts: *This isn't fair. I didn't do anything wrong. I can't believe that this is happening to me (especially with all that I've already gone through in my life). Just because they've got a lot of money doesn't mean that they can push people around and impose their will. Why can't things be flippin' easy for once? I'm a good person* (as if that had anything to do with it). I was in fear, in reaction, and desperately trying to find the justice and the meaning in all of it. I found it very difficult to get still and be present with the barrage of fear-based thoughts that was constantly storming my mind: *I just opened my own life coaching practice and spent tens of thousands of dollars on branding, advertising, my website, and P.R. for my new book, and now this? How am I going to be able to fund something like this? I didn't put enough savings aside for legal fees of this magnitude. Are you kidding me?*

My emotional landscape was kaleidoscopic. I found myself vacillating from acceptance and surrender to anxiety and terror. It was truly one of the most expansive rides of my life. One moment I'd be deeply still in meditation; the next moment I'd notice my irrational thoughts and behavior intensifying as I spent to excess, acted out through sex-capades, buried myself in longer work hours, and distracted myself with endless projects. Through it all, what I am most proud of is that I stood for myself and my truth. What I am most grateful for is that I gave myself the permission to ride the ride, as arduous as it was, and to learn as I went along. I will draw from that learning for decades to come.

Throughout our experience, my husband, Rhett, and

I knew that staying true to ourselves and adhering to our own truths would ensure that the situation would work out exactly as it was supposed to. And it did. The result was not what we had hoped or anticipated, but it worked out exactly the way it was supposed to. How do we know that? Because it resulted the way that it did; it couldn't have happened any other way. In short, all entities involved now coexist peacefully.

Rhett and I have always believed that everything is happening for our greater good. In our toughest moments, we did our best to draw from this faith. In the type of situation that could put a wedge in a relationship, our bond was strengthened. We came together in a way that we never had before. We learned how to be there for each other and how to really lean on each other. We became a very strong unit. We also learned that we can enjoy our lives regardless of the situation that lies before us and that we never have to be owned by the temporary circumstances that we are experiencing.

I was in my zenagogue for thirty-three months. I am proof that we can feel our way through and emerge with deeply broadened perspective, immense gratitude, and mindfulness that will enhance the rest of our lives.

27

WILLINGNESS

Many people have compulsive or addictive behavior patterns. As you come to see yourself with broadening perspective, you might see certain habits or behaviors differently. Pay attention to your motivations for any behavior in question. Behaviors that are addictive or compulsive will likely come to the forefront as you become more mindful and, thus, truthful with yourself. In order to intervene in our own addictive behavior, it is imperative that we observe ourselves. For our awareness alone allows us to clearly see the reality of its effects. Self-intervention requires the *willingness* to be honest with ourselves and others in regard to our thoughts and our behavior. We must give our feelings a voice, as well, as any repressed emotions can perpetuate more addictive behavior. It is crucial that we "pull our own covers". By fully disclosing how it really is for us, we begin to unburden ourselves of once-buried secrets, shame, and guilt.

In my experience, my willingness has been key to my sobriety from drugs and alcohol and my abstinence from compulsive eating and bulimarexia: my willingness to do what it takes; my willingness to be still; my willingness to venture inside; my willingness (and courage) to feel and express my emotions; my willingness to tell the truth and expose myself; my willingness to ask for help; my willingness to get to a meeting and to be part of a group; my willingness to work with a coach, counselor, or sponsor; my willingness to do the necessary excavation; my willingness to accept what is; my willingness to address the void inside of me; my willingness to challenge and alter my belief system; my willingness to explore different healing modalities; my willingness to forgive; my willingness to make amends; my willingness to surrender my will to be guided by a power greater than me. Willingness, to me, is the equivalent of investing into myself. It has afforded me a clean, open, and healthy life.

As I've grown in sobriety and consciousness, I've become less discriminatory of myself and more compassionate with myself. As a result, anytime I notice myself exhibiting any type of addictive or compulsive behavior, instead of labeling it as a problem, I prefer to be more merciful with myself by viewing it as a learning experience. This way, I'm much more present and available to receive guidance, support, and insight from my higher power. I begin by paying attention to how I feel before, during, and after I exhibit any behavior in question. I notice the thoughts perpetuating those feelings, and then I still my mind so that I can be open to discover what it is that I'm seeking in that addictive behavior. I invite you to apply this same method in your life. What are you seeking in your addictive behavior? Is it love? Comfort? Acceptance? Punishment? Making this connection will be transformative in your healing.

Case in point: for years, I engaged in sexual fetish behavior. Now for some people, that behavior is fun and adventurous; for me, it became obsessive and all-consuming. The rush was so intense that it honestly compared to being drunk or high. As much as I didn't want to admit it, that behavior started to become an integrity issue for me. Instead of stopping it cold turkey, I decided to bring more awareness to that compulsive behavior to learn from what it had to teach me.

I began by paying attention to my thoughts and the way I felt before, during, and after the encounters. I was very diligent about observing myself. In time, it became clearly evident that I was justifying and rationalizing behavior that I didn't feel right about exhibiting. The clever arguments that my frightened mind contrived in support of my acting out were astounding. However, there was one thing that I could no longer deny, and that was the exorbitant amount of anxiety that I would feel beforehand coupled with the overwhelming amount of disgust, shame, and deceitfulness that I would feel afterward. Thank God I slowed down long enough to notice those feelings and the knots in my stomach that were desperately trying to tell me that that behavior wasn't healthy for me.

It was shortly thereafter that I began to have greater comprehension as to what I had been seeking through my fetish adventures. Had you asked me at one point in my life if I could separate sex from love, I would've absolutely averred that sex and love were mutually exclusive. That belief not only authorized my behavior, but it also made it more challenging for me to discover what I was seeking in it. As I was driving away from one of those experiences, I recalled it as being very passionate, animalistic, and captivating. However, no fetish behavior had been involved. What it had included was an extraordinary amount of intimate connection. The fact that I had been satiated without engaging my fetish indicated that my compulsive behavior hadn't been about fulfilling my unique sexual needs as I had previously believed. Rather, it had been about fulfilling my *emotional* needs. In a profound moment of clarity on that drive home, I had the revelation that what I had actually been seeking in that behavior was *love*. This realization hit me hard and landed deep within me. I had been truly unaware of this. In my stillness on that beautiful spring afternoon, I made a connection on a cellular level that would profoundly alter the way I interact with myself.

Since that day, I haven't had the compulsion to escape

through that type of behavior. I attribute this to my willingness: my willingness to do the required excavation and the ongoing exploration that allows for me to live more consciously; my willingness to be more loving with myself; and my willingness to walk with God. So I ask you, how willing are you? What is it that you're looking for in any addictive or compulsive behavior that you display? What do you hope to find? Could it be time for you to make that connection for yourself?

28

WE ALL SHINE ON

I like to ask my clients, *Where are the places in your life that you shine?* Everybody has them. Where do you shine? Where in your life are you completely present, accessible, and in the zone of you? Where in your life do you find that your mind is quiet and that you're fully at peace? When do you feel the most connected to your higher power? Where are you the most creative or resourceful? Where in your life are you unbridled and free? Where do you feel that you're at your best? When do you feel the most alive? I ask my clients to be specific with their answers to this question, and I get many different responses, including: *painting, communing with nature, dancing, facilitating a workshop, riding my horse, running, cooking, litigating a case, lying on the couch with my spouse, spending time with my kids, doing yoga, troubleshooting, delivering a keynote speech, meditating, skiing, reminiscing with old friends, riding my motorcycle,* and so many more. Take a moment before you move on in this chapter to jot down the places in your life that you shine. Please be thorough and generous with yourself, and keep this list close by, should you ever need a reminder.

So I ask you, with all of the places where you've identified that you shine, how can it ever be definitive that you're not enough? It just doesn't add up. Here's the reality: it might be true that you don't *feel* enough at times. That's completely understandable, but it's also circumstantial. You can never be one hundred percent positive that you *are* not enough, because you've just identified numerous places in your life where you shine. This is unarguably indicative of the fact that you're *more* than enough. Give yourself a moment to let this sink in. I hope you can clearly see this.

There is a huge difference between not *being* enough and not *feeling* enough. Not being enough is a lie that we tell ourselves that prevents us from owning our power and keeps us beholden to our darkness instead of our light. It is one of the rationalizations we use to justify our actions or lack thereof. It's our go-to excuse for why our life is the way that it is. It's an easy fallback, but such an uneasy existence. When you're creating your life from a core foundation of not being enough, most everything in your life (including your loved ones) becomes contaminated by this belief. Your dissatisfaction spills over onto just about everyone and everything. It's nearly impossible to be truly satisfied.

There will be times in our lives when we don't feel enough. That is okay. The truth, however, is that we were made in the image and likeness of our creator. That divine consciousness is enough by definition. The fact that we were created in that image and likeness means that we are enough exactly as we are, too. We are innately whole beings. To dispute this would be to contradict our divine nature. Therefore, not being enough just isn't possible.

29

BULLY IN THE MIRROR

We are all, at this moment, living in a world where bullying is so prominent and commonplace that we barely even recognize it much of the time. It occurs more often and in so many more ways than we even realize. Consider tabloid journalism, gossip-focused news, reality television, celebrity-focused blogs, and many of the viral videos that we see on social networking sites, for instance. The bulk of their content fans the flames of conflict, prejudice, and discrimination. It feeds off of and exacerbates insecurities and feelings of fear and inadequacy. Now, I'm all for freedom of speech, absolutely. Personally, however, I just don't find it entertaining to read about or witness a person being ripped apart, shredded, or degraded. I don't find it humorous or enjoyable to watch another human being be the subject of humiliation because of their hairstyle, clothing, or size; for their missteps; or for whom they choose to love. I find heckling, bashing, shaming, ridiculing, or gossiping at another's expense all to be various forms of bullying. Can we not see the effects that this bullying is having on ourselves, on others, and on our children? Many have even taken their own lives because the humiliation, degradation, hopelessness, and despair were too painful to endure any longer.

It is imperative that we begin to pay attention to all of the socially accepted manners in which people are taunted and dehumanized, as they are insidious forms of bullying. For instance, many jokes, remarks, or funny quips, however harmless they may seem, are contributing to the bullying currently happening in our world. Now, I'm not saying that all one-liners are forms of bullying. I'm just saying that some are quite hurtful, pointed, and damaging and that we need to be accountable for the division that our words can create. As long as such displays are painted as socially acceptable, the harassment will continue. You have the power to choose whether or not to subscribe to or endorse it as entertainment.

What do you think our children are learning from all of the slanderous and discrediting behavior being exemplified by the adults on this planet? What are we teaching them? Is it any wonder when a child in elementary school pushes down another child? Is it a surprise when a junior high student ridicules others for their dialect, clothing, or their individuality? Why are we shocked when adolescents in high school are teased, harassed, or beaten because of their sexual orientation, their financial situation, or their appearance? How is any of this different from the very entertainment that so many adults choose to watch, laugh at, or emulate? Bullying of others by preying on their vulnerabilities takes countless forms. We are likely able to recognize a good number of them. However, we are very *unlikely* to notice one of the most common and most significant forms of bullying: the bullying of ourselves.

I believe that we bully ourselves through our nonacceptance and judgment of ourselves and our bodies. I also believe that neglecting, disrespecting, invalidating, or withholding from ourselves constitutes self-bullying. In addition, we're bullying us when we betray, blame, degrade, dismiss, reject, shame, or criticize ourselves. Our debasing internal monologues are yet another form of preying on our own vulnerabilities. May you begin to pay attention to how you speak about and treat yourself. It is imperative that we intervene and stop our own self-bullying. For in order for the bullying in the world to cease, the bullying of ourselves must do so first.

I have devised the following exercise to aid you in the expanded awareness of your own internal bullying. When embarking upon this journey, please find a quiet space that's free of distractions where you can get still, surrender, and allow your authentic truths from deep within to organically rise on their own.

You can do this exercise with a certain bully in mind or with everyone whom you consider to be a bully in your life. This examination is done in four phases so that you can thoroughly immerse yourself in each of them to ensure that you get the maximum benefit. Be as diligent as possible when completing this inventory. Do your best to *be with* whatever rises within you and to feel it. Surround yourself with lifelines if need be, as well. Please take your time, and do not read ahead. This exercise will serve you best if you complete each phase before advancing to the next.

Phase No. 1:

Write down the places, situations, or ways in which you've felt bullied and the name of the bully. For example: *Jack bullied me when he didn't listen to me.*

Phase No. 2:

Using your notes from Phase 1, substitute the words "I", "me", or "myself" in place of the names of your bullies or in any place where you've written the words "you", "they", "he", "she", etc. In addition, change the sentence to the present tense. For instance, if you've written the sentence: *Jack bullied me when he didn't listen to me,* your Phase 2 sentence would look like this: *I bully me when I don't listen to me.*

Some sentences, such as *Jack flirts with other*

women, won't work with the name substitutions. So in those cases, please write out how you *feel* or *felt* as a result of the bullying; for example: *I feel disrespected when Jack flirts with other women.* From there, please consider the ways in which you have treated yourself in a similar manner; for example: *I disrespect myself when I don't speak up for myself,* or *I disrespect myself when I invalidate my worth,* or *I disrespect myself when I tell myself that I'm not as attractive as those other women.* Feel free to take liberties with these sentences so that you may discover all the different ways that you treat yourself in kind. For instance, if you've written the sentence: *It was cruel of Jack to address my fat,* your Phase 2 sentence could look like this: *It was cruel to myself not to address Jack's comment,* or *I'm cruel to myself when I compare myself to another person,* or *It is cruel to myself not to appreciate my own beauty.*

If neither substituting you in place of the bully nor writing out how you feel when the bullying occurs suits your sentences from Phase 1, you might try the following:

1. Ask yourself: *What did that situation represent to me?* (e.g., being dismissed, being abandoned, being duped)

2. Ask yourself: *What feelings arise when I think about that situation?* (e.g., I feel disrespected; I feel rejected; I feel unappreciated)

3. Ask yourself: *What type of behavior was exemplified in my perception, interpretation, or experience of the situation?* (e.g., demeaning, abusive, cruel)

You can then take the answers to these questions and examine how you've behaved (or still behave) in the same ways toward yourself. For the above examples, for instance, think about when you might dismiss, disrespect, or act cruelly toward you. Please open your mind and excavate with compassion. These examples are not to indict or incriminate you. They are simply to provide you with a broadened perspective. If it's dismissive behavior that you're addressing, you might find that you dismiss yourself when you don't stand up for yourself. Perhaps you disrespect yourself when you discount your own beauty. Maybe you act cruelly toward yourself when you talk negatively about your body or when you smoke cigarettes. These are just suggestions to get you thinking. You will discover what is true for you.

This exercise is restorative and transformative. It will point you in the direction of what needs to be looked at, addressed, and excavated. If you really want to up the ante, let yourself take ownership of the times when you exemplify (or have exemplified) the same behaviors with others, as well: when you are dismissive of others, disrespectful toward others, or cruel toward others. Coming clean and telling the truth alters my perspective. In my experience, the realization that I sometimes display the same behavior that my bullies display humanizes not only me, but my bullies, as well. I see them in a different light. I have found that as I've grown in mercy and compassion for myself, I have grown in mercy and compassion for my bullies, as well. This allows me to live much more peacefully.

Phase No. 3:

Once you've related each instance to how you bully yourself, see if you can come up with some honest examples of how your self-bullying plays out in your life. If you're addressing the statement, *I disrespect myself when I discount my own beauty*, for example, you might come up with the following:

1. *Since I'm always comparing myself to others, I don't really know who I am, how great I am, or my innate worth.*
2. *I use it as my go-to excuse for why I'm not in a relationship, thus sustaining my fear that I'll never get married.*
3. *I live in a constant state of anxiety, but I put on a happy face to mask my pain, sadness, and despair, which zaps and depletes my life force, drive, and enthusiasm.*
4. *I grow suspicious of my spouse's female friends and acquaintances, which gets in the way of trusting and having deeper intimacy and connection with my spouse.*

Do this for each instance you've noted. When you're coming up with these examples, give yourself the permission to delve deeply without judgment. Let it all flow out of you without censoring anything. This portion of the exercise will specifically show you what needs attention and healing, and it will also provide invaluable insight as to why your life is exactly the way that it is.

Phase No. 4:

Now, review the sentences from Phase 2 that pertain to the ways you treat yourself along with the examples from Phase 3 of how they play out in your life. For each one, see if you can think of a tool that will help you to eradicate or neutralize your self-bullying. That way, you can be more merciful and loving with yourself. Below are some examples of tools you might choose to implement.

- Affirmations
- Prayer
- Aligning with your higher self
- Excavation work
- Journaling
- Seeking support
- Being forgiving with yourself
- Referring to yourself with reverence and kindness
- Accepting all as it is

- Acknowledging yourself
- Honoring your feelings and truth
- Challenging or altering your beliefs
- Having patience with yourself
- Nurturing the places in your life where you shine
- Focusing on what you *can* do and what *is* working
- Being honest
- Trusting yourself
- Maintaining authenticity
- Standing or speaking up for yourself
- Giving yourself permission to grieve
- Taking accountability
- Making amends with you whenever necessary
- Being willing
- Remaining loyal to yourself first
- Allowing yourself ample rest or alone time
- Living a balanced life
- Moving your body (e.g., yoga, walking, stretching, exercising)
- Meditating
- Celebrating you

You will undoubtedly encounter more bullies throughout your lifetime. May it benefit you to know that they enter your life bearing valuable lessons. They will continue to illuminate the areas of your life that need your attention.

They will show you what you have yet to make peace with and embrace. All you need do is be compassionate and merciful with yourself and always stay true to you. One day, you might actually perceive your bully as your aide.

30
NOTE TO SELF

I live knowing that I can change me, but that I cannot change others. I cannot change their behavior, their beliefs, their opinions, or their feelings. This would include: what they say; what they think; or how they feel about me, themselves, or anyone else. Lord knows, I've tried. What I've learned is that attempting to change another person into being who I want them to be (or into who *I* want to be) is futile. In addition, badgering or bullying another into somehow being different than they are is not only abusive to them, but also to me. Toiling in pursuit of such an impossible goal is an exhausting labor that very often results in animosity and exasperation. I stand to lose minutes, days, months, or even years when I'm trying to change another human being.

What I *can* change are my own perceptions, which can

alter the way I view, experience, feel about, and interact with others.

Throughout my lifetime, it has become evidently clear to me that my primary job is simply to love to the best of my ability. All that I can be is the best example of a loving being that I can. Gandhi didn't say, "Try to change people into being who you want them to be." He said, "Be the change you wish to see in the world." As always, the change begins with me.

31

LIFE IN FLUX

Loss of any kind can leave us feeling empty, distraught, or unsure of our place in the world. Losing your best friend, a loved one, a home that's been foreclosed upon, money in the stock market, or even a legal battle can be very challenging to make peace with. Perhaps your job has been terminated or your health has declined. Maybe you're lamenting the fact that you're aging, going through a breakup, or even suffering the loss of a piece of yourself. Surrendering and giving way to what is can help to alleviate your distress. I know that this might not be easy for you to do right now. That's understandable. Just remember that being in resistance to what is will only add to your suffering. Whereas, allowing the loss to be and accepting its actuality opens the space for us to move through it.

We might never understand the complexity of life, for

our world is just too great an enigma. May you find comfort in knowing that change is a constant. Everything is in perpetual transition, including ourselves. All is ephemeral, temporary, fleeting. If we can do our best to embrace the constant flux that is life and allow life to keep life-ing, we can have the most enriching journey.

32

MANIFEST

Can you think of a time when you felt so at peace, so present, so filled with love, and so pleased with where you were at the moment that you were struck with an overwhelming sense of fulfillment and gratitude? If you find it challenging to recall such a time, can you envision a situation that could occur in your future to put you in that state of pure bliss? It could be your upcoming wedding or holding your newborn baby. You might picture yourself at your dream vacation destination. Perhaps it's having all of your children and family gathered together at your home for the holidays. Or maybe it's hearing from your doctor that you've been restored to perfect health. Whatever the situation (whether it occurs in the past or the future), I implore you to discover it and to mentally put yourself in that moment as fully as you can, right now. Give yourself the permission to close your eyes and get still and to really explore that ideal scenario with every fiber of your being. What does it feel like to immerse yourself in such extreme happiness? Bringing this moment to life inside of you elevates your vibrational frequency. It puts you in a state of allowance, thus preparing you to be receptive and active in your manifestation process.

I do this by visualizing myself in the meditation room at the Casa de Dom Inacio in Abadiania, Brazil. I close my eyes, take in a few deep and conscious breaths, and I visualize myself seated comfortably in my favorite seat in the back pew of Current Room Number One. I can hear the footsteps and whispers of the people passing in front of me combined with the calming sound of the fan running behind me. I relish in the privilege and honor I feel while sitting current and aiding in others' quests for healing. In this place, my heart is wide open, and I can literally feel the power of God surging through me. I experience this love enveloping me, filling me, guiding me, and informing me. Being suspended in this state of grace is absolute elation for me. I relish the beauty, the silence, and the oneness that I experience. In my stillness, I am present, open, and allowing. I am vibrating at a high energetic frequency whereby all of my wishes may come to me, as I am accessible and available to receive them.

You can mentally place yourself in your own blissful space whenever you want to center yourself or amplify your manifestation process. All you need to do is relax into the moment, *presence* your vision, and allow it to unfold and take shape in your mind's eye. Sometimes, this takes practice so please be patient with yourself as you fine-tune this process and make it your own. It will be helpful to draw from your senses. Notice your surroundings within your visualization, for making it sensory rich will lead you deeper into the experience. It will behoove you to become familiar with all of the sensations associated with that euphoric space, as this is your *place of bliss*.

The more I immerse myself into that divine, open, tranquil space, the better I feel. The better I feel, the higher my vibration. The higher my vibration, the better equipped I am to magnetize my desires to me. That's the deal. That high energetic frequency is the place from which I begin my five-step creative process.

Here's how it works: the first step of this creative process is identifying and asking for what you want. Be specific. For this stage, simply specify *what* and *how much* of it you would like. It isn't up to you to figure out how it will or should make its way to you. It's not up to you to figure out the "how to". Leave that up to the universe or your higher power. This takes great trust, but all will come to you in its right and perfect time. I never obsess over *why* or *how* in this process, because that state of apprehension and exasperation only creates resistance and smothers, constructing a greater barrier between my desires and me. It's not about micro-managing and suffocating your vision. Simply focus on what it is that you would like to bring to your life. Remember, what you focus on expands.

The second step is to express gratitude to your higher power for your vision already being so. I simply say: *Thank you for [the having of something on its way]*. I know this may seem odd, because your desire is not here yet, but this is a great opportunity to apply your conviction and strengthen your faith. Since gratitude raises your vibrational frequency, it puts you in a primary position to receive.

The third step is to become quiet and still and to listen. I like to start this step with a statement: *Thank you for allowing me to be open and receptive to hear and to receive your wisdom and your guidance as it flows through me*. Always know that our requests are answered promptly with guidance. Now, by "promptly", I mean anywhere from within minutes to weeks. Your guidance could come in many forms: a phone call, a song, an advertisement, a gut instinct, a serendipitous event, or even a concept that pops into your mind. It is your job to stay alert and present. If you feel as though you're not receiving any guidance, you may be in a state of resistance. If this is the case, momentarily step off of the treadmill of life, and check in with yourself. If you're sensing any fear, address it.

The fourth step is to match your desires vibrationally, to feel just like you will feel once you have what you desire. In other words, stand at the finish line by feeling the having of that for which you aspire. Experience the joy, fulfillment, contentment, and elation of having it. Really breathe it in. Feel it the way you feel your place of bliss. In doing this, you are preparing your consciousness for its arrival. If you want to manifest a certain job, for example, see yourself shaking hands with your new employer; giving a presentation; or sitting at your new desk with your nameplate and your children's photo on it. Feel what it is like to be there, in that position. Immerse yourself in that visualization. Witnessing your desires alive in your imagination sets them in motion and allows for them to one day manifest.

The fifth and final step is simple, but not always easy. It, too, calls for great trust and surrender. Declare it to be so, then step away and patiently await its arrival while you get on with your life. All the while, know with conviction that your dreams and desires will arrive in their own sweet time. Within twelve weeks of implementing this process, I manifested my husband, whom I have now been with for over fourteen years.

33

Affirmative

There are many tools that can be instrumental in your creative process. With experimentation, you will discover those that work best for you. "I am" statements are one tool that I find to be incredibly empowering. I implement them every day. I find that once I declare them, I subsequently come into the having of them: *I am living a life that is better than I ever dreamed it could be; I am easy to support; I am safe; I am fearless; I am a joy to be around; I am free; I am at peace; I am perfect as I am; I am okay; I am well; I am always provided for; I am grateful; I am happy; I am healed; I am forgiving with myself and others; I am willing; I am alive; I am powerful beyond measure.* It's important to note that this process is not just about reciting a bunch of words or phrases and then blindly hoping they will come true. That is not how it works. This process is about connecting to your declaration and wholeheartedly feeling the having of it at the depths of your core. As you know, this takes steadfast presence, concentration, and conviction. The powers that be respond to the vibration that you are emitting, which is determined by your emotions. Just remember that the better you feel, the higher your vibrational frequency. So if you are feeling dispirited or finding it difficult to surrender to this process and to believe your declaration, try accessing your place of bliss. Your place of bliss can serve as an excellent transition into the space where you want to be when you begin this creative process.

Vision boards are another immensely helpful aid in your creation process. What I find so powerful and effective about my vision board is that, by keeping it in my line of sight, my intentions remain consistently at the forefront of my consciousness. Initially, I get still and journal out a very thorough written intention of what I desire: mentally, physically, spiritually, emotionally, financially, socially, occupationally, and in my life overall. Making this investment into myself sharpens my focus and leaves me clear. With my intention already alive and burning brightly inside of me, I begin to seek and construct physical representations in the form of images, items, words, or symbols that best represent what I desire. My collection symbolizes my relationship with God; ways of being; camaraderie, playfulness, celebration, and love, as well as my goals for health and vitality, my lifestyle, expanding my family, my career, future global humanitarian efforts, and so much more. In short, my vision board is loaded with loving inspiration that fuels my life. Every single piece on my vision board evokes a powerful energetic vibration from deep within me. Whenever I find something that really speaks to my heart, that embodies my life's purpose, and that is in line with my vision, I add it to my vision board. I urge you to do the same. A vision board can be created anywhere that you can keep a group of visual aids where you can see them all at once: a bulletin board, a refrigerator, an open wall. Add to it anything that sources you, inspires you, and calls forth your dreams and desires.

I've found that participating in activities that bring me pleasure also boosts my creative power. Anything that's kind to me and that's not an integrity issue raises my vibration, which allows for my desires to be manifested more quickly. I find pleasure in so many things: dancing, meditation, sitcoms, game nights, hiking, movies, yoga, prayer, vacations, spiritual retreats, listening to music, engaging in intimate conversations, sharing moments with family and friends, and even sitting on the couch at the end of the day with my husband. Where do you find pleasure? I invite you to welcome as much of it into your life as you can.

Perhaps the most extraordinarily powerful tools available to us are affirmations. Even though they might feel fake or phony at first, I encourage you to stick with them. You have the power to alter your inner commentary, which can be transformed with the help of your affirmations.

Implementing affirmations is the equivalent of planting seeds of new thoughts in our minds. Cultivated with our focus, connection, and conviction, they can yield a realization that has the power to generate a completely new way of living for us. To begin, consider what you would like to be true, and create an affirmation in line with it already being so. For instance: *I love and accept myself exactly as I am; All is okay; I love my life; I have complete financial freedom; It is okay to relax and do nothing; I believe in myself; I can laugh at myself and at life; My mind is clear and sharp; Love is kind; I enjoy my company; I listen; I treat myself with respect and loving kindness; Everything that I need is always supplied; My best is good enough; Delightful people seek out my services; Money flows to me easily and effortlessly; My body is beautiful; I move forward in my life confidently and enthusiastically; I express myself freely; Change is easy for me; I can do anything I want; Unexpected miracles happen for me every day; I revel in my uniqueness.* If you are finding it difficult to come up with affirmations that are personal to you, please call upon your higher power for support and guidance. Affirmations carry us to higher energetic frequencies so that we're more accessible to our intentions. Remember, it isn't about simply spouting a bunch of words by rote. It's about feeling the having of it from your core.

It is of vital importance that we fully commit to building and strengthening our mental muscle if we want to alter our lives. This might require asking your higher power for assistance. Bodybuilders create their physiques by committing to a disciplined regimen. They sculpt their muscles through hours and hours of practice, repetition, and consistency. They do not simply visit the gym a few times and then stop if they haven't seen the results that they were seeking. Instead, they focus on the outcome they're committed to achieving. They keep their eye on the prize, they stick with it, and they draw upon their faith and conviction. The same approach applies to building a stronger mental muscle. We derive the most benefit from a daily commitment. I recommend setting aside blocks of time each morning and evening to solidify your new beliefs.

Feel free to have fun with your affirmations and to be creative. You might want to make them into a poem, a song, a rhyme, or even a rap – whatever is most instrumental in helping you to connect to the new affirmative thoughts. Enjoy the process. May you find your own experience with affirmations to be enormously transformative.

34

PRAISE YOU

Acknowledgement is extremely nourishing for the soul. I find it to be for humans what water and sunlight are to plants. Despite its benefits, many people still find it quite challenging to give the gift of acknowledgment to themselves. This could be due to self-acknowledgment feeling uncomfortable or unfamiliar. Some people might not want to be perceived as conceited or as braggarts. Others might not even know that acknowledging oneself is an option. Self-acknowledgment can be one of the highest applications of self-love. It's okay to acknowledge, praise, and celebrate yourself. Whether you feel as though you've earned it or that you're deserving of it, it is your right, and it is essential to your evolvement.

When we can acknowledge, praise, and celebrate ourselves, we no longer feel the need to seek that from our partners. We no longer expect them to give us something that we haven't yet been able to give to ourselves (and, therefore, something that we were incapable of truly receiving, as well). In nourishing and nurturing ourselves, we take back responsibility for our own happiness, contentedness, and satisfaction, as we're no longer relying upon someone else. We get to have a whole different experience when we can appreciate and champion ourselves and our efforts.

If this concept is foreign to you, and you're unsure how to go about appreciating yourself, begin with self-acknowledgment for the victories in your life. This can be as simple as telling yourself: *you're amazing, great job, you really went for it, congratulations,* or *look what you can do.* Such acknowledgments can be employed for both your big victories as well as your small ones. You will likely find that you have many more of them than you realized. Finishing a project, receiving a promotion, buying a new car, or refinancing your home are more obvious victories. Grieving a loss or even just feeling an uncomfortable feeling that you once before might have suppressed or avoided is a victory that might go unacknowledged. Perhaps you've enforced a boundary, stood up for yourself, spoken your truth, or faced an addiction. Maybe you've confronted a part of yourself about which you were in denial or a part of your life that wasn't working for you. Something as simple as being attentive, considerate, and patient with yourself can be victorious, as well. Self-acknowledgment is a game changer. It has the capability to lift us, ignite us, soothe us, and comfort us. The power of acknowledgment is undeniable.

35

CLEAN LISTENING

Though relationships can be effortless at times, they can also be quite challenging. I've had some of my greatest learning through my relationships, as I know that they are meant to educate me, awaken me, and aid in my evolution. Through much trial and error, I've come to learn that partners never want a lecture; they simply want to be heard. They want to know that what they're saying has merit, is important, and is valued and acknowledged. If you want to foster more intimacy, trust, and connection in your relationships, one of the best tools that you can employ is listening.

Listening is one of the greatest ways that we can serve not only ourselves, but also one another. The degree to which we can listen and really hear what another human being is saying will be reflected directly in our friendships, partnerships, and relationships. When people have been truly listened to and not judged or reprimanded, they leave the encounter knowing that what they expressed was received, valued, and acknowledged. This immensely shifts the dynamic of the relationship by creating more safety and trust. In the absence of barriers and defenses, we find more warmth, affection, and understanding in our relationships, as well. With a stronger foundation of trust, more intimacy, playfulness, and connection can be explored.

It is important that we pay attention to how (and from which beliefs) we listen. Do you listen openly, lovingly, and receptively where others feel heard, safe, and accepted in your company? Or, do you listen aggressively, judgmentally, or defensively where people might fear you or feel emotionally unsafe around you? Observe yourself. Do you interrupt when someone is sharing? Do you steamroll conversations? Do you already know what you're going to say before someone else finishes speaking? If so, are you really listening? Are you present or even available for conversation? Which beliefs are you adhering to in that moment that are keeping you from being open and accessible?

You might be listening from a belief that you're inferior, where you feel as though you're wrong or bad or deficient in some way. This could manifest as you often being apologetic, or you might end up being argumentative or defensive, or thinking you are always right. If the latter is the case, could you be trying to compensate for your feelings of lack in hopes that others won't discover this? Might that also allow you to feel as though you have power or control? You might be listening in a righteous or superior way, where you frequently find yourself saying *I know*, or *I knew that*. This would spawn from some part of you feeling threatened, or you wouldn't feel the need to deflect in this way (and try to throw others off the scent of how you often feel about yourself). Can you see how this isolates you and detaches you from the conversation? How might this directly affect your relationships? I'm not bringing up these examples so that you feel bad about yourself. On the contrary, I want to help you create more awareness as to how (and from which beliefs) you listen so that your relationships may have more connection, trust, and fun.

In addition, pay attention to what you hear and how you hear it after someone has spoken. What was your interpretation of what was said? For example, when your loved one says to you, "I'd really appreciate it if you could make more of an effort to be on time," it could be a clean comment, where they're just taking care of themselves and letting you know what they prefer. Maybe they're trying to let you in, and they're not trying to control you or tell you what to do. Perhaps there is no hidden meaning. They could just be making a loving attempt to close a gap and be closer with you. However, if you're adhering to the belief that you're inadequate, then, regardless of what's said, you're probably going to hear that you're at fault in some way: your best is never good enough; you always disappoint them; you've done something wrong; you can never get it right; you can never please them; once again you've let them down; and so on. Could it be possible that what you heard was different than what was actually said? Could it be possible that there was no insinuation or tone in the delivery? Could it also be possible that what you heard (and how you heard it) was filtered through your frightened mind and its belief system? If this is possible, then maybe what you heard was not what was said and instead was just your interpretation. The other person could simply have been making a direct and honest remark or request to bring you in closer, but because of the thoughts that you're in agreement with, you've contorted what they actually said to fit your belief system. If you're having any sort of a reaction, you might want to investigate that. Now I'm not saying that hurtful or upsetting things can't be said. We all know that they can. I just want you to look at your side of the fence so that you get to have the type of relationships that you desire. Your reaction may indicate that you could benefit from doing some internal excavation that would enable you to be more present and accessible in future exchanges. Your presence would then transcend into your ability to really listen and hear what others are trying to convey, which allows for more closeness and harmony in your relationships.

what's been lodged inside of us to begin to jostle free. As dormant feelings rise to the surface, just know that it is part of the process, and it's an indicator that you're right on track. Remember to surround yourself with lifelines, and allow yourself to be with any feelings that arise.

Once you have fully articulated your grievances, you can liberate yourself further by mentally placing yourself in the shoes of the person whom you'd like to forgive. What type of childhood did they have? What were their formative years like? What were their parents like? How did they learn to communicate? What were they taught about life, family, nurturing? How were they taught to treat themselves? What was their example of how to feel and express their feelings? Which ethics were imparted upon them? What life experiences have they endured? What did they learn about love? Really take a moment or two to contemplate what it might be like to have had their past and their experiences. Consider how those factors shaped the beliefs that they adhere to that dictate their actions, behavior, and reactions. It's quite revelatory to have this understanding, because it can make the other person's actions less inconceivable. Each of us is working with the level of consciousness that we have. Knowing this, it's easier to comprehend, based upon a person's thoughts, beliefs, and life experiences, why they do, act, and behave as they do. May it console you to know that abuse and maltreatment are results of another's internal torment spilling outward. With this knowledge, may the perceived personal nature of it all begin to lift and fade away. When one is conscious, one would never impose their will on, or harm, another.

Now let's take a look at you. This will be most conducive to your emancipation if you look carefully and are one hundred percent honest. Think of the ways in which you've displayed the same type of behavior as the person you would like to forgive. Now these examples don't have to be exact reenactments of the situations you experienced. They're just examples of where and how you've exhibited similar behavior, even if it showed up in a different form or to a different degree. Take a moment to ponder this, or feel free to make a list. While searching, I ask that you think back throughout the entirety of your life and not just the recent past. If you would like to forgive someone for being absent when you were a child, can you think of a time when you weren't there for another or when you weren't there for yourself? Maybe you'd like to forgive someone for being cruel, abusive, or punishing. If so, can you find the times in your life when you've been cruel, abusive, or punishing to another or to yourself?

Now consider the level of consciousness from which you were operating at the time. Didn't you have to do exactly as you did, the way that you did it? In fact, haven't you always done the best that you could with the tools that you had in that moment and the beliefs that were mandating your behavior and actions? I would venture to say that you have. Then isn't it possible that the person whom you'd like to forgive has also been doing the best that they could with their beliefs, tools, and consciousness level? Again, I'm not implying that what happened was okay. I'm simply hoping that this perspective will alleviate more suffering.

How could forgiveness enrich your life? What would forgiveness make room for in your life? As we open and expand our minds, our perspectives broaden. In this grace, we find more compassion, mercy, and space for ourselves, which transcends onto those we'd like to forgive. When this occurs, you won't have to actively work at forgiving another. The forgiveness will happen naturally on its own.

37

A Greater World

An interpersonal exchange can be an intoxicating spiritual elixir. This goes for every intercommunication that we have the opportunity to share with another human being, no matter how inconsequential it might seem in the moment. The smallest gesture of connection can leave an imprint in one's world. Experience this for yourself. Devote a morning to extending a warm greeting to each person you encounter, and witness the effect that your heartfelt generosity has upon other human beings. That instance of benevolence has the potential to lift one's spirits, to brighten one's day, and to warm another's soul. Kindness works like a chain reaction. Once extended, its effects are exponential.

We never know what someone else is going through. That moment of connection you share with them may be the catalyst that alters the trajectory of their day. Whether

39

THE POWER OF LAUGHTER

Some of my dearest friends can attest to the fact that laughing and having fun are a huge part of my life. I even bring that playfulness into my client sessions when appropriate, for I find laughter to be therapeutic. We can sometimes take ourselves and our lives so seriously that we miss out on the opportunity in the moment before us. By easing up on ourselves and laughing at our own humanity, we get to experience an entirely new world. When we come to recognize the absurdity and the humor in the thoughts we have about situations that once troubled us, we initiate a new relationship with ourselves and with life, one that is much more lighthearted and far more joyous. This raises our energetic vibration, thus drawing more goodness and ease into our lives. When we can laugh, genuinely and sincerely laugh, at the way things have played out in our lives, along with our participation throughout, we prepare the space for a magnanimous existence. Laughter is powerful. It is healing and rejuvenating in so many ways and on so many levels. It is one of the greatest natural exhilarators available to us.

The beauty of uncensored laughter is that it feels so wonderful. The bonus is that it automatically draws us into the present moment. Laughter keeps us in that moment and only that moment. We can't be anywhere else. When we're laughing, we're allowing our being to be fully enveloped by joy. Joyful laughter is its own place of bliss. It naturally places us in a state of allowance. The energy emanating from within us becomes invigorating and intoxicating. Think back to the last time that you laughed uncontrollably and what that felt like in your body, in your soul. Remember how surrendered you were. How did it affect the moments that followed?

Each time you erupt with laughter, notice how it infuses and nourishes every cell in your body. It's infectious and contagious. Watch the way it welcomes and engages others. I have witnessed kind humor and laughter disarm and unite, as they soften barriers and supersede differences.

40

THE WAY IN

I gift myself with meditation daily, and I find that it has a profound effect on my psyche and how I am able to function in my daily life. The advantage in meditation, for me, is that it clears away my anxiety and stress while it calmly centers me in a state of peacefulness. I use meditation as a way to ground myself, to heal any imbalances in my life, and as a way to connect to my true self. Meditation offers me a pure, open space from which to listen for guidance and direction. I am very grateful for that sacred and blissful realm from which I receive insights that aid in the creation of my life. Surrendering myself in meditation also allows me the benefit of self-discovery and the resulting inspiration that accompanies that. Meditation is my way of laying a direct pipeline to the divine.

Many of my clients and friends have told me that they

find it difficult to meditate, because they are unable to relax into the meditation due to the barrage of thoughts that are constantly bombarding their minds. That chatter makes it challenging to focus and leads to frustration, which often deters people from pursuing meditation any further. I completely understand. However, meditation isn't about controlling, blocking, or pushing away our thoughts. There is no need to create discomfort within by "fighting" for stillness. Meditation is about allowing; it is about allowing all to be as it is in that moment, period. Thus, all you need to do is get still, allow any feelings or thoughts to arise, and just do your best to allow them to pass through you. Patience and practice are key. Please call upon your higher power for support, should you require it.

John Kabat Zinn compares a thought to a soap bubble that forms, begins to float up and away, and inevitably pops, just as your thought forms, travels through your mind, and inevitably disappears. Simply surrender into the state of your mind as it is in each and every moment. By allowing your thoughts to run their course, they will naturally cease with time and presence.

My own meditation ritual begins with playing some soft, meditative music, as I find that it centers and relaxes me. Steven Halpern's "Gifts of the Angels" and Eckhart Tolle's "Music for Inner Stillness" are two of my favorites. Next, it's about getting comfortable. So sometimes I'm sitting upright in a foam seat with a back cushion, and

41

THANKSGIVING

One of the greatest things that you can do for yourself today to have the most transformative effect upon your life is to consciously express gratitude for what you appreciate that exists in your life at this moment. I understand how challenging this can seem at times; however, acknowledging the blessings that are currently present in your life alters your perceptions, which profoundly influence your perspective and, thus, the way that you experience life. For your benefit, take a moment to recognize all of the blessings for which you're grateful right now. It might be your health or shared moments with the special people in your life. Maybe you're grateful for your connection to your higher power, for your sobriety, for the ability to exercise, for your state of contentment, for your mental clarity, for the mentors in your life, that it was only a fender bender, or for having a free moment to relax and do something for yourself. You might find yourself appreciative of something as simple as your car starting, having your basic needs met, the wonder of nature, a kind message from someone who appreciates you, or your pets playing together. Or, it could be a gift as crucial as having the medicine for your ailment that evokes gratitude within you.

I hope that you can see that there's always something for which to be grateful. There is something to acknowledge in your life, at all times, small as it might seem. One beneficial investment into solidifying your awareness of this fact is to comprise a gratitude journal. Each morning and evening, take a moment to write down a few of the things that you were thankful for that day. I find this to be important, because once you begin to realize the true blessings in your life, you pay attention in a different way. You begin to notice things that before might have been overlooked or taken for granted: someone holding an elevator for you or being graciously greeted by the security guard at the bank, for example. Your awareness becomes heightened. This newfound vision can dramatically shift your exchanges with others as well as the way you are able to maneuver in life. In addition, chronicling all for which you're appreciative allows you to continuously see more and more of the gifts that you live amid. Your gratitude journal serves as a list of irrefutable examples that illustrate the beauty, the goodness, and the decency that surround you, while also proving that the universe is friendly and supportive.

As you are well aware, life keeps "life-ing". As such, there may be times that seem bleak, when you feel as though there's nothing to be grateful for in your life. If you find yourself at such an impasse, please just pause for a moment, get as still as you can, and ask yourself, *What can I be authentically grateful for in this moment?* If you've been feeling sad, then maybe you can be grateful for the awareness of your sadness. If you've just lost a loved one, you might be grateful for the time you shared with such a wonderful person. Or, you might be grateful for finding the ability to put one foot in front of the other and move forward. Maybe you can appreciate the fact that you have the capacity to acknowledge feelings of loneliness or despair today rather than trying to escape them. You might simply find yourself grateful that you're willing to look inside and tell the truth about what you find.

Gratitude lands us in a better feeling place, one where we enjoy our lives a whole lot more. It raises our vibrational frequency, allowing for more goodness and love to be drawn to us. When we're living gratefully, we're naturally open and receptive to the unlimited generosity of the universe. The more that we can find to appreciate, the more the universe will bestow upon us to appreciate. To enhance your quality of life, begin by recognizing and appreciating all of the wonderful blessings that surround you right now at this very moment.

42

ALL RESPLENDENT

I wholeheartedly believe that we are all interconnected, as we are all a part of the divine whole from which we came. Therefore, that divine grace, magnificence, and omnipotence resides in every one of us. Love, peacefulness, joy, and beauty live within every person, as well. This luminosity exists in everything: within us, as us, and all around us. It is inherent in our being. Look where we originated. This means that the greatness for which we often strive also already exists within us. We are comprised of that magnificence. It's not something to attain; it's something that's simply a given. It is innate and ever present. End of story. No proof required.

It is truly invigorating to be in the presence of a person who is emanating their luminous essence. To me, there is nothing more incandescent and radiant than a heart in full bloom, one that is welcoming and uninhibited. I find it overwhelmingly powerful to witness that ever-flowing stream of divine love igniting the hearts of others and inspiring us to live in oneness.

You are pure magnificence. You are perfect, beautiful, and whole exactly as you are. May you forever stay true to the light that you are, allowing it to beam in full expression.

About The Author

Michael Blomsterberg loves to reacquaint people with their innate greatness. He is a spiritual teacher who has been working in the greater Los Angeles community for over 25 years. He earned his Master Certified Life Coach designation from Coach For Life, an International Coaching Federation (ICF)-approved program. Michael's mission is to synergize his extensive life experience with his professional training so to aid others in the enhancement of their lives. He draws from his self-created Michael Blomsterberg Life Coaching Enlightened Living Model (ELM) when working with clients and conveys its tools further through his public and media appearances. A known and respected facilitator in countless local recovery facilities and support groups, Michael also continues to work closely with organizations throughout the U.S. and the world.

www.michaelblomsterberg.com